Eagles Over the Trenches

Eagles Over
the Trenches

Two First Hand Accounts of
the American Escadrille at
War in the Air During
World War 1

Flying For France
With the American Escadrille at Verdun

by James R. McConnell

Our Pilots in the Air

by William B. Perry

LEONAUR

Eagles Over the Trenches: Two First Hand Accounts of the American Escadrille at War in the Air During World War 1

Flying For France
With the American Escadrille at Verdun
by James R. McConnell

Our Pilots in the Air
by William B. Perry

Published by Leonaur Ltd in 2007

Text in this form and material original to this edition
copyright © 2007 Leonaur Ltd

ISBN: 978-1-84677-267-2 (hardcover)
ISBN: 978-1-84677-268-9 (softcover)

http://www.leonaur.com

Contents

Flying for France

Introduction   11
Verdun   13
Verdun to the Somme   45
Letters From Sergeant McConnell—At The Front   62
How France Trains Pilot Aviators   70
Against Odds   77

Our Pilots in the Air

A Bombing Air Raid   91
The Whir of Wings   97
Fighting Both Enemy and Elements   105
Winning Promotions   113
The Practice Drill   122
Catching the Spy   129
Downing the Sausages   138
Blaine's Further Adventures   146
The Final Fight   155
The Battles in the Air   171
The Adventures of Erwin   179
At the Ruined Chateau   187
Two Perilous Night Trips   198
Making Ready for Another Forward Drive   207
The Conflict   215
Buck and the Boche Aloft   224
Back Home   233
Conclusion   242

Flying for France
With the American Escadrille at Verdun

by James R. McConnell

To Mrs. Alice S. Weeks

Who having lost a splendid son in
the French Army has given to a great
number of us other Americans in
the war the tender sympathy
and help of a mother.

Introduction

One day in January, 1915, I saw Jim McConnell in front of the Court House at Carthage, North Carolina. "Well," he said, "I'm all fixed up and am leaving on Wednesday."

"Where for?" I asked.

"I've got a job to drive an ambulance in France," was his answer.

And then he went on to tell me, first, that as he saw it the greatest event in history was going on right at hand and that he would be missing the opportunity of a lifetime if he did not see it.

"These Sand Hills," he said "will be here forever, but the war won't; and so I'm going." Then, as an afterthought, he added: "And I'll be of some use, too, not just a sight-seer looking on; that wouldn't be fair."

So he went. He joined the American ambulance service in the Vosges, was mentioned more than once in the orders of the day for conspicuous bravery in saving wounded under fire, and received the much-coveted Croix de Guerre.

Meanwhile, he wrote interesting letters home. And his point of view changed, even as does the point of view of all Americans who visit Europe. From the attitude of an adventurous spirit anxious to see the excitement, his letters showed a new belief that any one who goes to France and is not able and willing to do more than his share—to give everything in him toward helping the wounded and suffering—has no business there.

And as time went on, still a new note crept into his letters; the first admiration for France was strengthened and almost replaced by a new feeling—a profound conviction that France and the French people were fighting the fight of liberty against enormous odds. The new spirit of France—the spirit of the "Marseillaise," strengthened by a grim determination and absolute certainty of being right—pervades every line he writes. So he gave up the ambulance service and enlisted in the French flying corps along with an ever-increasing number of other Americans.

The spirit which pervades them is something above the spirit of adventure that draws many to war; it is the spirit of a man who has found an inspiring duty toward the advancement of liberty and humanity and is glad and proud to contribute what he can.

His last letters bring out a new point—the assurance of victory of a just cause. "Of late," he writes, "things are much brighter and one can feel a certain elation in the air. Victory, before, was a sort of academic certainty; now, it is felt."

F. C. P.
November 10, 1916.

CHAPTER 1

Verdun

Beneath the canvas of a huge hangar mechanicians are at work on the motor of an airplane. Outside, on the borders of an aviation field, others loiter awaiting their aerial charge's return from the sky. Near the hangar stands a hut-shaped tent. In front of it several short-winged biplanes are lined up; inside it three or four young men are lolling in wicker chairs.

They wear the uniform of French army aviators. These uniforms, and the grim-looking machine guns mounted on the upper planes of the little aircraft, are the only warlike note in a pleasantly peaceful scene. The war seems very remote. It is hard to believe that the greatest of all battles—Verdun—rages only twenty-five miles to the north, and that the field and hangars and mechanicians and aviators and airplanes are all playing a part therein.

Suddenly there is the distant hum of a motor. One of the pilots emerges from the tent and gazes fixedly up into the blue sky. He points, and one glimpses a black speck against the blue, high overhead. The sound of the motor ceases, and the speck grows larger. It moves earthward in steep dives and circles, and as it swoops closer, takes on the shape of an airplane. Now one can make out the red, white, and blue circles under the wings which mark a French war-plane, and the distinctive insignia of the pilot on its sides.

"*Ton patron arrive!*" one mechanician cries to another. "Your boss is coming!"

The machine dips sharply over the top of a hangar, straightens out again near the earth at a dizzy speed a few feet above it and, losing momentum in a surprisingly short time, hits the ground with tail and wheels. It bumps along a score of yards and then, its motor whirring again, turns, rolls toward the hangar, and stops. A human form, enveloped in a species of garment for all the world like a diver's suit, and further adorned with goggles and a leather hood, rises unsteadily in the cockpit, clambers awkwardly overboard and slides down to terra firma.

A group of soldiers, enjoying a brief holiday from the trenches in a cantonment near the field, straggle forward and gather timidly about the airplane, listening open-mouthed for what its rider is about to say.

"Hell!" mumbles that gentleman, as he starts divesting himself of his flying garb.

"What's wrong now?" inquires one of the tenants of the tent.

"Everything, or else I've gone nutty," is the indignant reply, delivered while disengaging a leg from its Teddy Bear trousering. "Why, I emptied my whole roller on a Boche this morning, point blank at not fifteen metres off. His machine gun quit firing and his propeller wasn't turning and yet the darn fool just hung up there as if he were tied to a cloud. Say, I was so sure I had him it made me sore—felt like running into him and yelling, 'Now, you fall, you bum!'"

The eyes of the *poilus* register surprise. Not a word of this dialogue, delivered in purest American, is intelligible to them. Why is an aviator in a French uniform speaking a foreign tongue, they mutually ask themselves. Finally one of them, a little chap in a uniform long since bleached of its horizon-blue colour by the mud of the firing line, whisperingly interrogates a mechanician as to the identity of these strange air folk.

"But they are the Americans, my old one," the latter explains with noticeable condescension.

Marvelling afresh, the infantrymen demand further details. They learn that they are witnessing the return of the American Escadrille—composed of Americans who have volunteered to fly for France for the duration of the war—to their station near Bar-le-Duc, twenty-five miles south of Verdun, from a flight over the battle front of the Meuse. They have barely had time to digest this knowledge when other dots appear in the sky, and one by one turn into airplanes as they wheel downward. Finally all six of the machines that have been aloft are back on the ground and the American Escadrille has one more sortie over the German lines to its credit.

PERSONNEL OF THE ESCADRILLE

Like all worth-while institutions, the American Escadrille, of which I have the honour of being a member, was of gradual growth. When the war began, it is doubtful whether anybody anywhere envisaged the possibility of an American entering the French aviation service. Yet, by the fall of 1915, scarcely more than a year later, there were six Americans serving as full-fledged pilots, and now, in the summer of 1916, the list numbers fifteen or more, with twice that number training for their pilot's license in the military aviation schools.

The pioneer of them all was William Thaw, of Pittsburgh, who is to-day the only American holding a commission in the French flying corps. Lieutenant Thaw, a flyer of considerable reputation in America before the war, had enlisted in the Foreign Legion in August, 1914. With considerable difficulty he had himself transferred, in the early part of 1915, into aviation, and the autumn of that year found him piloting a Caudron biplane, and doing excellent observation work. At the same time, Sergeants Norman Prince, of Boston, and Elliot Cowdin, of New York—who were the first to enter the aviation service coming directly from the United States—were at the front on Voisin planes with a cannon mounted in the bow.

Sergeant Bert Hall, who signs from the Lone Star State and had got himself shifted from the Foreign Legion to aviation soon after Thaw, was flying a Nieuport fighting machine, and, a little later, instructing less-advanced students of the air in the Avord Training School. His particular chum in the Foreign Legion, James Bach, who also had become an aviator, had the distressing distinction soon after he reached the front of becoming the first American to fall into the hands of the enemy. Going to the assistance of a companion who had broken down in landing a spy in the German lines, Bach smashed his machine against a tree. Both he and his French comrade were captured, and Bach was twice court-martialed by the Germans on suspicion of being an American *franc-tireur*—the penalty for which is death! He was acquitted but of course still languishes in a prison camp "somewhere in Germany." The sixth of the original sextet was Adjutant Didier Masson, who did exhibition flying in the States until—Carranza having grown ambitious in Mexico—he turned his talents to spotting *los Federales* for General Obregon. When the real war broke out, Masson answered the call of his French blood and was soon flying and fighting for the land of his ancestors.

Of the other members of the escadrille Sergeant Givas Lufbery, American citizen and soldier, but dweller in the world at large, was among the earliest to wear the French airman's wings. Exhibition work with a French pilot in the Far East prepared him efficiently for the task of patiently unloading explosives on to German military centres from a slow-moving Voisin which was his first mount. Upon the heels of Lufbery came two more graduates of the Foreign Legion—Kiffin Rockwell, of Asheville, N.C., who had been wounded at Carency; Victor Chapman, of New York, who after recovering from his wounds became an airplane bomb-dropper and so caught the craving to become a pilot. At about this time one Paul Pavelka, whose birthplace was Madison, Conn., and who from the age of fifteen had sailed the seven seas, managed to slip out of the Foreign Legion into aviation and joined the other Americans at Pau.

There seems to be a fascination to aviation, particularly when it is coupled with fighting. Perhaps it's because the game is new, but more probably because as a rule nobody knows anything about it. Whatever be the reason, adventurous young Americans were attracted by it in rapidly increasing numbers. Many of them, of course, never got fascinated beyond the stage of talking about joining. Among the chaps serving with the American ambulance field sections a good many imaginations were stirred, and a few actually did enlist, when, toward the end of the summer of 1915, the Ministry of War, finding that the original American pilots had made good, grew more liberal in considering applications.

Chouteau Johnson, of New York; Lawrence Rumsey, of Buffalo; Dudley Hill, of Peekskill, N.Y.; and Clyde Balsley, of El Paso; one after another doffed the ambulance driver's khaki for the horizon-blue of the French flying corps. All of them had seen plenty of action, collecting the wounded under fire, but they were all tired of being non-combatant spectators. More or less the same feeling actuated me, I suppose. I had come over from Carthage, N.C., in January, 1915, and worked with an American ambulance section in the Bois-le-Prêtre. All along I had been convinced that the United States ought to aid in the struggle against Germany. With that conviction, it was plainly up to me to do more than drive an ambulance. The more I saw the splendour of the fight the French were fighting, the more I felt like an *embusqué*—what the British call a "shirker." So I made up my mind to go into aviation.

A special channel had been created for the reception of applications from Americans, and my own was favourably replied to within a few days. It took four days more to pass through all the various departments, sign one's name to a few hundred papers, and undergo the physical examinations. Then I was sent to the aviation depot at Dijon and fitted out with a uniform and personal equipment. The next stop was the school at Pau, where I was to be taught to fly. My elation at arriving there was second only to my satisfaction at being a French soldier. It was a vast improvement, I thought, in the American Ambulance.

Talk about forming an all-American flying unit, or escadrille, was rife while I was at Pau. What with the pilots already breveted, and the *élèves*, or pupils in the training-schools, there were quite enough of our compatriots to man the dozen airplanes in one escadrille. Every day somebody "had it absolutely straight" that we were to become a unit at the front, and every other day the report turned out to be untrue. But at last, in the month of February, our dream came true. We learned that a captain had actually been assigned to command an American escadrille and that the Americans at the front had been recalled and placed under his orders. Soon afterward we *élèves* got another delightful thrill.

Three Types of French Air Service

Thaw, Prince, Cowdin, and the other veterans were training on the Nieuport! That meant the American Escadrille was to fly the Nieuport—the best type of *avion de chasse*—and hence would be a fighting unit. It is necessary to explain parenthetically here that French military aviation, generally speaking, is divided into three groups—the *avions de chasse* or airplanes of pursuit, which are used to hunt down enemy aircraft or to fight them off; *avions de bombardmente,* big, unwieldy monsters for use in bombarding raids; and *avions de réglage,* cumbersome creatures designed to regulate artillery fire, take photographs, and do scout duty. The Nieuport is the smallest, fastest-rising, fastest-moving biplane in the French service. It can travel 110 miles an hour, and is a one-man apparatus with a machine gun mounted on its roof and fired by the pilot with one hand while with the other and his feet he operates his controls. The French call their

Nieuport pilots the "aces" of the air. No wonder we were tickled to be included in that august brotherhood!

Before the American Escadrille became an established fact, Thaw and Cowdin, who had mastered the Nieuport, managed to be sent to the Verdun front. While there Cowdin was credited with having brought down a German machine and was proposed for the *Médaille Militaire,* the highest decoration that can be awarded a non-commissioned officer or private.

After completing his training, receiving his military pilot's brevet, and being perfected on the type of plane he is to use at the front, an aviator is ordered to the reserve headquarters near Paris to await his call. Kiffin Rockwell and Victor Chapman had been there for months, and I had just arrived, when on the 16th of April orders came for the Americans to join their escadrille at Luxeuil, in the Vosges.

The rush was breathless! Never were flying clothes and fur coats drawn from the quartermaster, belongings packed, and red tape in the various administrative bureaus unfurled, with such headlong haste. In a few hours we were aboard the train, panting, but happy. Our party consisted of Sergeant Prince, and Rockwell, Chapman, and myself, who were only corporals at that time. We were joined at Luxeuil by Lieutenant Thaw and Sergeants Hall and Cowdin.

For the veterans our arrival at the front was devoid of excitement; for the three neophytes—Rockwell, Chapman, and myself—it was the beginning of a new existence, the entry into an unknown world. Of course Rockwell and Chapman had seen plenty of warfare on the ground, but warfare in the air was as novel to them as to me. For us all it contained unlimited possibilities for initiative and service to France, and for them it must have meant, too, the restoration of personality lost during those months in the trenches with the Foreign Legion. Rockwell summed it up characteristically.

"Well, we're off for the races," he remarked.

There is a considerable change in the life of a pilot when he arrives on the front. During the training period he is subject to rules and regulations as stringent as those of the barracks. But once assigned to duty over the firing line he receives the treatment accorded an officer, no matter what his grade. Save when he is flying or on guard, his time is his own. There are no roll calls or other military frills, and in place of the bunk he slept upon as an *élève*, he finds a regular bed in a room to himself, and the services of an orderly. Even men of higher rank who although connected with his escadrille are not pilots, treat him with respect. His two mechanicians are under his orders. Being volunteers, we Americans are shown more than the ordinary consideration by the ever-generous French Government, which sees to it that we have the best of everything.

On our arrival at Luxeuil we were met by Captain Thénault, the French commander of the American Escadrille—officially known as No. 124, by the way—and motored to the aviation field in one of the staff cars assigned to us. I enjoyed that ride. Lolling back against the soft leather cushions, I recalled how in my apprenticeship days at Pau I had had to walk six miles for my laundry.

The equipment awaiting us at the field was even more impressive than our automobile. Everything was brand new, from the fifteen Fiat trucks to the office, magazine, and rest tents. And the men attached to the escadrille! At first sight they seemed to outnumber the Nicaraguan army—mechanicians, chauffeurs, armourers, motorcyclists, telephonists, wireless operators, Red Cross stretcher bearers, clerks! Afterward I learned they totalled seventy-odd, and that all of them were glad to be connected with the American Escadrille.

In their hangars stood our trim little Nieuports. I looked mine over with a new feeling of importance and gave orders to my mechanicians for the mere satisfaction of being able to. To find oneself the sole proprietor of a fighting airplane is quite a treat, let me tell you. One gets accustomed to it, though, after one has used up two or three of them—at the French Government's expense.

Rooms were assigned to us in a villa adjoining the famous hot baths of Luxeuil, where Caesar's cohorts were wont to besport themselves. We messed with our officers, Captain Thénault and Lieutenant de Laage de Mieux, at the best hotel in town. An automobile was always on hand to carry us to the field. I began to wonder whether I was a summer resorter instead of a soldier.

Among the pilots who had welcomed us with open arms, we discovered the famous Captain Happe, commander of the Luxeuil bombardment group. The doughty bomb-dispenser, upon whose head the Germans have set a price, was in his quarters. After we had been introduced, he pointed to eight little boxes arranged on a table.

"They contain *Croix de Guerre* for the families of the men I lost on my last trip," he explained, and he added: "It's a good thing you're here to go along with us for protection. There are lots of Boches in this sector."

I thought of the luxury we were enjoying: our comfortable beds, baths, and motor cars, and then I recalled the ancient custom of giving a man selected for the sacrifice a royal time of it before the appointed day.

To acquaint us with the few places where a safe landing was possible we were motored through the Vosges Mountains and on into Alsace. It was a delightful opportunity to see that glorious countryside, and we appreciated it the more because we knew its charm would be lost when we surveyed it from the sky. From the air the ground presents no scenic effects. The ravishing beauty of the Val d'Ajol, the steep mountain sides bristling with a solid mass of giant pines, the myriads of glittering cascades tumbling downward through fairylike avenues of verdure, the roaring, tossing torrent at the foot of the slope—all this loveliness, seen from an airplane at 12,000 feet, fades into flat splotches of green traced with a tiny ribbon of silver.

The American Escadrille was sent to Luxeuil primarily to acquire the team work necessary to a flying unit. Then, too, the new pilots needed a taste of anti-aircraft artillery to familiarize them with the business of aviation over a battlefield. They shot well in that sector, too. Thaw's machine was hit at an altitude of 13,000 feet.

The Escadrille's First Sortie

The memory of the first sortie we made as an escadrille will always remain fresh in my mind because it was also my first trip over the lines. We were to leave at six in the morning. Captain Thénault pointed out on his aerial map the route we were to follow. Never having flown over this region before, I was afraid of losing myself. Therefore, as it is easier to keep other airplanes in sight when one is above them, I began climbing as rapidly as possible, meaning to trail along in the wake of my companions. Unless one has had practice in flying in formation, however, it is hard to keep in contact. The diminutive *avions de chasse* are the merest pinpoints against the great sweep of landscape below and the limitless heavens above. The air was misty and clouds were gathering. Ahead there seemed a barrier of them. Although as I looked down the ground showed plainly, in the distance everything was hazy. Forging up above the mist, at 7,000 feet, I lost the others altogether. Even when they are not closely joined, the clouds, seen from immediately above, appear as a solid bank of white. The spaces between are indistinguishable. It is like being in an Arctic ice field.

To the south I made out the Alps. Their glittering peaks projected up through the white sea about me like majestic icebergs. Not a single plane was visible anywhere, and I was growing very uncertain about my position. My splendid isolation had become oppressive, when, one by one, the others began bobbing up above the cloud level, and I had company again.

We were over Belfort and headed for the trench lines. The cloud banks dropped behind, and below us we saw the smiling plain of Alsace stretching eastward to the Rhine. It was distinctly pleasurable, flying over this conquered land. Following the course of the canal that runs to the Rhine, I sighted, from a height of 13,000 feet over Dannemarie, a series of brown, woodworm-like tracings on the ground—the trenches!

Shrapnel that Couldn't be Heard

My attention was drawn elsewhere almost immediately, however. Two balls of black smoke had suddenly appeared close to one of the machines ahead of me, and with the same disconcerting abruptness similar balls began to dot the sky above, below, and on all sides of us. We were being shot at with shrapnel. It was interesting to watch the flash of the bursting shells, and the attendant smoke puffs—black, white, or yellow, depending on the kind of shrapnel used. The roar of the motor drowned the noise of the explosions. Strangely enough, my feelings about it were wholly impersonal.

We turned north after crossing the lines. Mulhouse seemed just below us, and I noted with a keen sense of satisfaction our invasion of real German territory. The Rhine, too, looked delightfully accessible. As we continued northward I distinguished the twin lakes of Gérardmer sparkling in their emerald setting. Where the lines crossed the Hartmannsweilerkopf there were little spurts of brown smoke as shells burst in the trenches. One could scarcely pick out the old city of Thann from among the numerous neighbouring villages, so tiny it seemed in the valley's mouth. I had never been higher than 7,000 feet and was unaccustomed to reading country from a great altitude. It was also bitterly cold, and even in my fur-lined combination I was shivering. I noticed, too, that I had to take long, deep breaths in the rarefied atmosphere. Looking downward at a certain angle, I saw what at first I took to be a round, shimmering pool of water. It was simply the effect of the sunlight on the congealing mist. We had been keeping an eye out for German machines since leaving our lines, but none had shown up. It wasn't surprising, for we were too many.

Only four days later, however, Rockwell brought down the escadrille's first plane in his initial aerial combat. He was flying alone when, over Thann, he came upon a German on reconnaissance. He dived and the German turned toward his own lines, opening fire from a long distance. Rockwell kept straight after him. Then, closing to within thirty yards, he pressed on the release of his machine gun, and saw the enemy gunner fall backward and the pilot crumple up sideways in his seat. The plane flopped downward and crashed to earth just behind the German trenches. Swooping close to the ground Rockwell saw its debris burning away brightly. He had turned the trick with but four shots and only one German bullet had struck his Nieuport. An observation post telephoned the news before Rockwell's return, and he got a great welcome. All Luxeuil smiled upon him—particularly the girls. But he couldn't stay to enjoy his popularity. The escadrille was ordered to the sector of Verdun.

While in a way we were sorry to leave Luxeuil, we naturally didn't regret the chance to take part in the aerial activity of the world's greatest battle. The night before our departure some German aircraft destroyed four of our tractors and killed six men with bombs, but even that caused little excitement compared with going to Verdun. We would get square with the Boches over Verdun, we thought—it is impossible to chase airplanes at night, so the raiders made a safe getaway.

Off to Verdun

As soon as we pilots had left in our machines, the trucks and tractors set out in convoy, carrying the men and equipment. The Nieuports carried us to our new post in a little more than an hour. We stowed them away in the hangars and went to have a look at our sleeping quarters. A commodious villa half way between the town of Bar-le-Duc and the aviation field had been assigned to us, and comforts were as plentiful as at Luxeuil.

Our really serious work had begun, however, and we knew it. Even as far behind the actual fighting as Bar-le-Duc one could sense one's proximity to a vast military operation. The endless convoys of motor trucks, the fast-flowing stream of troops, and the distressing number of ambulances brought realization of the near presence of a gigantic battle.

Within a twenty-mile radius of the Verdun front aviation camps abound. Our escadrille was listed on the schedule with the other fighting units, each of which has its specified flying hours, rotating so there is always an *escadrille de chasse* over the lines. A field wireless to enable us to keep track of the movements of enemy planes became part of our equipment.

Lufbery joined us a few days after our arrival. He was followed by Johnson and Balsley, who had been on the air guard over Paris. Hill and Rumsey came next, and after them Masson and Pavelka. Nieuports were supplied them from the nearest depot, and as soon as they had mounted their instruments and machine guns, they were on the job with the rest of us. Fifteen Americans are or have been members of the American Escadrille, but there have never been so many as that on duty at any one time.

Battles in the Air

Before we were fairly settled at Bar-le-Duc, Hall brought down a German observation craft and Thaw a Fokker. Fights occurred on almost every sortie. The Germans seldom cross into our territory, unless on a bombarding jaunt, and thus practically all the fighting takes place on their side of the line. Thaw dropped his Fokker in the morning, and on the afternoon of the same day there was a big combat far behind the German trenches. Thaw was wounded in the arm, and an explosive bullet detonating on Rockwell's wind-shield tore several gashes in his face. Despite the blood which was blinding him Rockwell managed to reach an aviation field and land. Thaw, whose wound bled profusely, landed in a dazed condition just within our lines. He was too weak to walk, and French soldiers carried him to a field dressing-station, whence he was sent to Paris for further treatment. Rockwell's wounds were less serious and he insisted on flying again almost immediately.

A week or so later Chapman was wounded. Considering the number of fights he had been in and the courage with which he attacked it was a miracle he had not been hit before. He always fought against odds and far within the enemy's country. He flew more than any of us, never missing an opportunity to go up, and never coming down until his gasoline was giving out. His machine was a sieve of patched-up bullet holes. His nerve was almost superhuman and his devotion to the cause for which he fought sublime. The day he was wounded he attacked four machines. Swooping down from behind, one of them, a Fokker, riddled Chapman's plane. One bullet cut deep into his scalp, but Chapman, a master pilot, escaped from the trap, and fired several shots to show he was still safe. A stability control had been severed by a bullet. Chapman held the broken rod in one hand, managed his machine with the other, and succeeded in landing on a near-by aviation field. His wound was dressed, his machine repaired, and he immediately took the air in pursuit of some more enemies. He would take no rest, and with bandaged head continued to fly and fight.

The escadrille's next serious encounter with the foe took place a few days later. Rockwell, Balsley, Prince, and Captain Thénault were surrounded by a large number of Germans, who, circling about them, commenced firing at long range. Realizing their numerical inferiority, the Americans and their commander sought the safest way out by attacking the enemy machines nearest the French lines. Rockwell, Prince, and the captain broke through successfully, but Balsley found himself hemmed in. He attacked the German nearest him, only to receive an explosive bullet in his thigh. In trying to get away by a vertical dive his machine went into a corkscrew and swung over on its back. Extra cartridge rollers dislodged from their case hit his arms. He was tumbling straight toward the trenches, but by a supreme effort he regained control, righted the plane, and landed without disaster in a meadow just behind the firing line.

Soldiers carried him to the shelter of a near-by fort, and later he was taken to a field hospital, where he lingered for days between life and death. Ten fragments of the explosive bullet were removed from his stomach. He bore up bravely, and became the favourite of the wounded officers in whose ward he lay. When we flew over to see him they would say: *Il est un brave petit gars, l'aviateur Américain,* (He's a brave little fellow, the American aviator.) On a shelf by his bed, done up in a handkerchief, he kept the pieces of bullet taken out of him, and under them some sheets of paper on which he was trying to write to his mother, back in El Paso.

Balsley was awarded the *Médaille Militaire* and the *Croix de Guerre,* but the honours scared him. He had seen them decorate officers in the ward before they died.

CHAPMAN'S LAST FIGHT

Then came Chapman's last fight. Before leaving, he had put two bags of oranges in his machine to take to Balsley, who liked to suck them to relieve his terrible thirst, after the day's flying was over. There was an aerial struggle against odds, far within the German lines, and Chapman, to divert their fire from his comrades, engaged several enemy airmen at once. He sent one tumbling to earth, and had forced the others off when two more swooped down upon him. Such a fight is a matter of seconds, and one cannot clearly see what passes. Lufbery and Prince, whom Chapman had defended so gallantly, regained the French lines. They told us of the combat, and we waited on the field for Chapman's return. He was always the last in, so we were not much worried. Then a pilot from another fighting escadrille telephoned us that he had seen a Nieuport falling. A little later the observer of a reconnaissance airplane called up and told us how he had witnessed Chapman's fall. The wings of the plane had buckled, and it had dropped like a stone he said.

We talked in lowered voices after that; we could read the pain in one another's eyes. If only it could have been some one else, was what we all thought, I suppose. To lose Victor was not an irreparable loss to us merely, but to France, and to the world as well. I kept thinking of him lying over there, and of the oranges he was taking to Balsley. As I left the field I caught sight of Victor's mechanician leaning against the end of our hangar. He was looking northward into the sky where his *patron* had vanished, and his face was very sad.

PROMOTIONS AND DECORATIONS

By this time Prince and Hall had been made adjutants, and we corporals transformed into sergeants. I frankly confess to a feeling of marked satisfaction at receiving that grade in the world's finest army. I was a far more important person, in my own estimation, than I had been as a second lieutenant in the militia at home. The next impressive event was the awarding of decorations. We had assisted at that ceremony for Cowdin at Luxeuil, but this time three of our messmates were to be honoured for the Germans they had brought down. Rockwell and Hall received the *Médaille Militaire* and the *Croix de Guerre,* and Thaw, being a lieutenant, the *Légion d'honneur* and another "palm" for the ribbon of the *Croix de Guerre* he had won previously. Thaw, who came up from Paris specially for the presentation, still carried his arm in a sling.

There were also decorations for Chapman, but poor Victor, who so often had been cited in the Orders of the Day, was not on hand to receive them.

Our daily routine goes on with little change. Whenever the weather permits—that is, when it isn't raining, and the clouds aren't too low—we fly over the Verdun battlefield at the hours dictated by General Headquarters. As a rule the most successful sorties are those in the early morning.

We are called while it's still dark. Sleepily I try to reconcile the French orderly's muttered, *C'est l'heure, monsieur,* that rouses me from slumber, with the strictly American words and music of *When that Midnight Choo Choo Leaves for Alabam* warbled by a particularly wide-awake pilot in the next room. A few minutes later, having swallowed some coffee, we motor to the field. The east is turning grey as the hangar curtains are drawn apart and our machines trundled out by the mechanicians. All the pilots whose planes are in commission—save those remaining behind on guard—prepare to leave. We average from four to six on a sortie, unless too many flights have been ordered for that day, in which case only two or three go out at a time.

Now the east is pink, and overhead the sky has changed from grey to pale blue. It is light enough to fly. We don our fur-lined shoes and combinations and adjust the leather flying hoods and goggles. A good deal of conversation occurs—perhaps because, once aloft, there's nobody to talk to.

"Eh, you," one pilot cries jokingly to another, "I hope some Boche just ruins you this morning, so I won't have to pay you the fifty francs you won from me last night!"

This financial reference concerns a poker game.

"You do, do you?" replies the other as he swings into his machine. "Well, I'd be glad to pass up the fifty to see you landed by the Boches. You'd make a fine sight walking down the street of some German town in those wooden shoes and pyjama pants. Why don't you dress yourself? Don't you know an aviator's supposed to look *chic?*"

A sartorial eccentricity on the part of one of our colleagues is here referred to.

The raillery is silenced by a deafening roar as the motors are tested. Quiet is briefly restored, only to be broken by a series of rapid explosions incidental to the trying out of machine guns. You loudly inquire at what altitude we are to meet above the field.

"Fifteen hundred metres—go ahead!" comes an answering yell.

Essence et gaz! (Oil and gas!) you call to your mechanician, adjusting your gasoline and air throttles while he grips the propeller.

Contact! he shrieks, and *Contact!* you reply. You snap on the switch, he spins the propeller, and the motor takes. Drawing forward out of line, you put on full power, race across the grass and take the air. The ground drops as the hood slants up before you and you seem to be going more and more slowly as you rise. At a great height you hardly realize you are moving. You glance at the clock to note the time of your departure, and at the oil gauge to see its throb. The altimeter registers 650 feet. You turn and look back at the field below and see others leaving.

In three minutes you are at about 4,000 feet. You have been making wide circles over the field and watching the other machines. At 4,500 feet you throttle down and wait on that level for your companions to catch up. Soon the escadrille is bunched and off for the lines. You begin climbing again, gulping to clear your ears in the changing pressure. Surveying the other machines, you recognize the pilot of each by the marks on its side—or by the way he flies. The distinguishing marks of the Nieuports are various and sometimes amusing. Bert Hall, for instance, has BERT painted on the left side of his plane and the same word reversed (as if spelled backward with the left hand) on the right—so an aviator passing him on that side at great speed will be able to read the name without difficulty, he says!

The country below has changed into a flat surface of vari-coloured figures. Woods are irregular blocks of dark green, like daubs of ink spilled on a table; fields are geometrical designs of different shades of green and brown, forming in composite an ultra-cubist painting; roads are thin white lines, each with its distinctive windings and crossings—from which you determine your location. The higher you are the easier it is to read.

In about ten minutes you see the Meuse sparkling in the morning light, and on either side the long line of sausage-shaped observation balloons far below you. Red-roofed Verdun springs into view just beyond. There are spots in it where no red shows and you know what has happened there. In the green pasture land bordering the town, round flecks of brown indicate the shell holes. You cross the Meuse.

Verdun, Seen from the Sky

Immediately east and north of Verdun there lies a broad, brown band. From the Woevre plain it runs westward to the "S" bend in the Meuse, and on the left bank of that famous stream continues on into the Argonne Forest. Peaceful fields and farms and villages adorned that landscape a few months ago—when there was no Battle of Verdun. Now there is only that sinister brown belt, a strip of murdered Nature. It seems to belong to another world. Every sign of humanity has been swept away. The woods and roads have vanished like chalk wiped from a blackboard; of the villages nothing remains but grey smears where stone walls have tumbled together. The great forts of Douaumont and Vaux are outlined faintly, like the tracings of a finger in wet sand. One cannot distinguish any one shell crater, as one can on the pockmarked fields on either side. On the brown band the indentations are so closely interlocked that they blend into a confused mass of troubled earth. Of the trenches only broken, half-obliterated links are visible.

Columns of muddy smoke spurt up continually as high explosives tear deeper into this ulcered area. During heavy bombardment and attacks I have seen shells falling like rain. The countless towers of smoke remind one of Gustave Doré's picture of the fiery tombs of the arch-heretics in Dante's "Hell." A smoky pall covers the sector under fire, rising so high that at a height of 1,000 feet one is enveloped in its mist-like fumes. Now and then monster projectiles hurtling through the air close by leave one's plane rocking violently in their wake. Airplanes have been cut in two by them.

The Roar Of Battle—Unheard

For us the battle passes in silence, the noise of one's motor deadening all other sounds. In the green patches behind the brown belt myriads of tiny flashes tell where the guns are hidden; and those flashes, and the smoke of bursting shells, are all we see of the fighting. It is a weird combination of stillness and havoc, the Verdun conflict viewed from the sky.

Far below us, the observation and range-finding planes circle over the trenches like gliding gulls. At a feeble altitude they follow the attacking infantrymen and flash back wireless reports of the engagement. Only through them can communication be maintained when, under the barrier fire, wires from the front lines are cut. Sometimes it falls to our lot to guard these machines from Germans eager to swoop down on their backs. Sailing about high above a busy flock of them makes one feel like an old mother hen protecting her chicks.

"Navigating" in a Sea of Clouds

The pilot of an *avion de chasse* must not concern himself with the ground, which to him is useful only for learning his whereabouts. The earth is all-important to the men in the observation, artillery-regulating, and bombardment machines, but the fighting aviator has an entirely different sphere. His domain is the blue heavens, the glistening rolls of clouds below the fleecy banks towering above, the vague aerial horizon, and he must watch it as carefully as a navigator watches the storm-tossed sea.

On days when the clouds form almost a solid flooring, one feels very much at sea, and wonders if one is in the navy instead of aviation. The diminutive Nieuports skirt the white expanse like torpedo boats in an arctic sea, and sometimes, far across the cloud-waves, one sights an enemy escadrille, moving as a fleet.

Principally our work consists of keeping German airmen away from our lines, and in attacking them when opportunity offers. We traverse the brown band and enter enemy territory to the accompaniment of an antiaircraft cannonade. Most of the shots are wild, however, and we pay little attention to them. When the shrapnel comes uncomfortably close, one shifts position slightly to evade the range. One glances up to see if there is another machine higher than one's own. Low and far within the German lines are several enemy planes, a dull white in appearance, resembling sand flies against the mottled earth. High above them one glimpses the mosquito-like forms of two Fokkers. Away off to one side white shrapnel puffs are vaguely visible, perhaps directed against a German crossing the lines. We approach the enemy machines ahead, only to find them slanting at a rapid rate into their own country. High above them lurks a protection plane. The man doing the "ceiling work," as it is called, will look after him for us.

Tactics of an Air Battle

Getting started is the hardest part of an attack. Once you have begun diving you're all right. The pilot just ahead turns tail up like a trout dropping back to water, and swoops down in irregular curves and circles. You follow at an angle so steep your feet seem to be holding you back in your seat. Now the black Maltese crosses on the German's wings stand out clearly.

You think of him as some sort of big bug. Then you hear the rapid tut-tut-tut of his machine gun. The man that dived ahead of you becomes mixed up with the topmost German. He is so close it looks as if he had hit the enemy machine. You hear the staccato barking of his *mitrailleuse* and see him pass from under the German's tail.

The rattle of the gun that is aimed at you leaves you undisturbed. Only when the bullets pierce the wings a few feet off do you become uncomfortable. You see the gunner crouched down behind his weapon, but you aim at where the pilot ought to be—there are two men aboard the German craft—and press on the release hard. Your *mitrailleuse* hammers out a stream of bullets as you pass over and dive, nose down, to get out of range. Then, hopefully, you re-dress and look back at the foe. He ought to be dropping earthward at several miles a minute. As a matter of fact, however, he is sailing serenely on. They have an annoying habit of doing that, these Boches.

Rockwell, who attacked so often that he has lost all count, and who shoves his machine gun fairly in the faces of the Germans, used to swear their planes were armoured. Lieutenant de Laage, whose list of combats is equally extensive, has brought down only one. Hall, with three machines to his credit, has had more luck. Lufbery, who evidently has evolved a secret formula, has dropped four, according to official statistics, since his arrival on the Verdun front. Four "palms"—the record for the escadrille, glitter upon the ribbon of the *Croix de Guerre* accompanying his *Médaille Militaire*. (Footnote: This book was written in the fall of 1915. Since that time many additional machines have been credited to the American flyers.)

A pilot seldom has the satisfaction of beholding the result of his bull's-eye bullet. Rarely—so difficult it is to follow the turnings and twistings of the dropping plane—does he see his fallen foe strike the ground. Lufbery's last direct hit was an exception, for he followed all that took place from a balcony seat. I myself was in the "nigger-heaven," so I know. We had set out on a sortie together just before noon, one August day, and for the first time on such an occasion had lost each other over the lines. Seeing no Germans, I passed my time hovering over the French observation machines. Lufbery found one, however, and promptly brought it down. Just then I chanced to make a southward turn, and caught sight of an airplane falling out of the sky into the German lines.

As it turned over, it showed its white belly for an instant, then seemed to straighten out, and planed downward in big zigzags. The pilot must have gripped his controls even in death, for his craft did not tumble as most do. It passed between my line of vision and a wood, into which it disappeared. Just as I was going down to find out where it landed, I saw it again skimming across a field, and heading straight for the brown band beneath me. It was outlined against the shell-racked earth like a tiny insect, until just northwest of Fort Douaumont it crashed down upon the battlefield. A sheet of flame and smoke shot up from the tangled wreckage. For a moment or two I watched it burn; then I went back to the observation machines.

I thought Lufbery would show up and point to where the German had fallen. He failed to appear, and I began to be afraid it was he whom I had seen come down, instead of an enemy. I spent a worried hour before my return homeward. After getting back I learned that Lufbery was quite safe, having hurried in after the fight to report the destruction of his adversary before somebody else claimed him, which is only too frequently the case. Observation posts, however, confirmed Lufbery's story, and he was of course very much delighted. Nevertheless, at luncheon, I heard him murmuring, half to himself: "Those poor fellows."

The German machine gun operator, having probably escaped death in the air, must have had a hideous descent. Lufbery told us he had seen the whole thing, spiralling down after the German. He said he thought the German pilot must be a novice, judging from his manoeuvres. It occurred to me that he might have been making his first flight over the lines, doubtless full of enthusiasm about his career. Perhaps, dreaming of the Iron Cross and his Gretchen, he took a chance—and then swift death and a grave in the shell-strewn soil of Douaumont.

Generally the escadrille is relieved by another fighting unit after two hours over the lines. We turn homeward, and soon the hangars of our field loom up in the distance. Sometimes I've been mighty glad to see them and not infrequently I've concluded the pleasantest part of flying is just after a good landing. Getting home after a sortie, we usually go into the rest tent, and talk over the morning's work. Then some of us lie down for a nap, while others play cards or read. After luncheon we go to the field again, and the man on guard gets his chance to eat. If the morning sortie has been an early one, we go up again about one o'clock in the afternoon. We are home again in two hours and after that two or three energetic pilots may make a third trip over the lines. The rest wait around ready to take the air if an enemy bombardment group ventures to visit our territory—as it has done more than once over Bar-le-Duc. False alarms are plentiful, and we spend many hours aloft squinting at an empty sky.

Prince's Aerial Fireworks

Now and then one of us will get ambitious to do something on his own account. Not long ago Norman Prince became obsessed with the idea of bringing down a German "sausage," as observation balloons are called. He had a special device mounted on his Nieuport for setting fire to the aerial frankfurters. Thus equipped he resembled an advance agent for Payne's fireworks more than an *aviateur de chasse*. Having carefully mapped the enemy "sausages," he would sally forth in hot pursuit whenever one was signalled at a respectable height. Poor Norman had a terrible time of it! Sometimes the reported "sausages" were not there when he arrived, and sometimes there was a super-abundance of German airplanes on guard.

He stuck to it, however, and finally his appetite for "sausage" was satisfied. He found one just where it ought to be, swooped down upon it, and let off his fireworks with all the gusto of an American boy on the Fourth of July. When he looked again, the balloon had vanished. Prince's performance isn't so easy as it sounds, by the way. If, after the long dive necessary to turn the trick successfully, his motor had failed to retake, he would have fallen into the hands of the Germans.

After dark, when flying is over for the day, we go down to the villa for dinner. Usually we have two or three French officers dining with us besides our own captain and lieutenant, and so the table talk is a mixture of French and English. It's seldom we discuss the war in general. Mostly the conversation revolves about our own sphere, for just as in the navy the sea is the favourite topic, and in the army the trenches, so with us it is aviation. Our knowledge about the military operations is scant. We haven't the remotest idea as to what has taken place on the battlefield—even though we've been flying over it during an attack—until we read the papers; and they don't tell us much.

Frequently pilots from other escadrilles will be our guests in passing through our sector, and through these visitations we keep in touch with the aerial news of the day, and with our friends along the front. Gradually we have come to know a great number of *pilotes de chasse*. We hear that so-&-so has been killed, that some one else has brought down a Boche and that still another is a prisoner.

We don't always talk aviation, however. In the course of dinner almost any subject may be touched upon, and with our cosmopolitan crowd one can readily imagine the scope of the conversation. A Burton Holmes lecture is weak and watery compared to the travel stories we listen to. Were O. Henry alive, he could find material for a hundred new yarns, and William James numerous pointers for another work on psychology, while De Quincey might multiply his dreams *ad infinitum*. Doubtless alienists as well as fiction writers would find us worth studying. In France there's a saying that to be an aviator one must be a bit "off."

After dinner the same scene invariably repeats itself, over the coffee in the "next room." At the big table several sportive souls start a poker game, while at a smaller one two sedate spirits wrap themselves in the intricacies of chess. Captain Thénault labours away at the mess room piano, or in lighter mood plays with Fram, his police dog. A phonograph grinds out the ancient query "Who Paid the Rent for Mrs. Rip Van Winkle?" or some other ragtime ditty. It is barely nine, however, when the movement in the direction of bed begins.

A few of us remain behind a little while, and the talk becomes more personal and more sincere. Only on such intimate occasions, I think, have I ever heard death discussed. Certainly we are not indifferent to it. Not many nights ago one of the pilots remarked in a tired way:

"Know what I want? Just six months of freedom to go where and do what I like. In that time I'd get everything I wanted out of life, and be perfectly willing to come back and be killed."

Then another, who was about to receive 2,000 francs from the American committee that aids us, as a reward for his many citations, chimed in.

"Well, I didn't care much before," he confessed, "but now with this money coming in I don't want to die until I've had the fun of spending it."

So saying, he yawned and went up to bed.

JAMES R. McCONNELL

AMERICANS WHO ARE FLYING FOR FRANCE

TWO MEMBERS OF THE AMERICAN ESCADRILLE
WHO WERE KILLED

WHISKEY THE LION, THE MASCOT OF THE
AMERICAN FLYING SQUADRON IN FRANCE

KIFFIN ROCKWELL, KILLED IN AN AIR DUEL OVER VERDUN

Sergeant Lufbery in one of the new Nieuports

CHAPTER 2

Verdun to the Somme

On the 12th of October, twenty small airplanes flying in a V formation, at such a height they resembled a flock of geese, crossed the river Rhine, where it skirts the plains of Alsace, and, turning north, headed for the famous Mauser works at Oberndorf. Following in their wake was an equal number of larger machines, and above these darted and circled swift fighting planes. The first group of aircraft was flown by British pilots, the second by French and three of the fighting planes by Americans in the French Aviation Division. It was a cosmopolitan collection that effected that successful raid.

We American pilots, who are grouped into one escadrille, had been fighting above the battlefield of Verdun from the 20th of May until orders came the middle of September for us to leave our airplanes, for a unit that would replace us, and to report at Le Bourget, the great Paris aviation centre.

The mechanics and the rest of the personnel left, as usual, in the escadrille's trucks with the material. For once the pilots did not take the aerial route but they boarded the Paris express at Bar-le-Duc with all the enthusiasm of schoolboys off for a vacation. They were to have a week in the capital! Where they were to go after that they did not know, but presumed it would be the Somme. As a matter of fact the escadrille was to be sent to Luxeuil in the Vosges to take part in the Mauser raid.

Besides Captain Thénault and Lieutenant de Laage de Mieux, our French officers, the following American pilots were in the escadrille at this time: Lieutenant Thaw, who had returned to the front, even though his wounded arm had not entirely healed; Adjutants Norman Prince, Hall, Lufbery, and Masson; and Sergeants Kiffin Rockwell, Hill, Pavelka, Johnson, and Rumsey. I had been sent to a hospital at the end of August, because of a lame back resulting from a smash up in landing, and couldn't follow the escadrille until later.

Every aviation unit boasts several mascots. Dogs of every description are to be seen around the camps, but the Americans managed, during their stay in Paris, to add to their menagerie by the acquisition of a lion cub named "Whiskey." The little chap had been born on a boat crossing from Africa and was advertised for sale in France. Some of the American pilots chipped in and bought him. He was a cute, bright-eyed baby lion who tried to roar in a most threatening manner but who was blissfully content the moment one gave him one's finger to suck. "Whiskey" got a good view of Paris during the few days he was there, for some one in the crowd was always borrowing him to take him some place. He, like most lions in captivity, became acquainted with bars, but the sort "Whiskey" saw were not for purposes of confinement.

The orders came directing the escadrille to Luxeuil and bidding farewell to gay "Paree" the men boarded the Belfort train with bag and baggage—and the lion. Lions, it developed, were not allowed in passenger coaches. The conductor was assured that "Whiskey" was quite harmless and was going to overlook the rules when the cub began to roar and tried to get at the railwayman's finger. That settled it, so two of the men had to stay behind in order to crate up "Whiskey" and take him along the next day.

The escadrille was joined in Paris by Robert Rockwell, of Cincinnati, who had finished his training as a pilot, and was waiting at the Reserve (Robert Rockwell had gone to France to work as a surgeon in one of the American war hospitals. He disliked remaining in the rear and eventually enlisted in aviation).

The period of training for a pilot, especially for one who is to fly a fighting machine at the front, has been very much prolonged. It is no longer sufficient that he learns to fly and to master various types of machines. He now completes his training in schools where aerial shooting is taught, and in others where he practises combat, group manoeuvres, and acrobatic stunts such as looping the loop and the more difficult tricks. In all it requires from seven to nine months.

Dennis Dowd, of Brooklyn, N.Y., is so far the only American volunteer aviator killed while in training. Dowd, who had joined the Foreign Legion, shortly after the war broke out, was painfully wounded during the offensive in Champagne. After his recovery he was transferred, at his request, into aviation. At the Buc school he stood at the head of the fifteen Americans who were learning to be aviators, and was considered one of the most promising pilots in the training camp. On August 11, 1916, while making a flight preliminary to his brevet, Dowd fell from a height of only 260 feet and was instantly killed. Either he had fainted or a control had broken.

While a patient at the hospital Dowd had been sent packages by a young French girl of Neuilly. A correspondence ensued, and when Dowd went to Paris on convalescent leave he and the young lady became engaged. He was killed just before the time set for the wedding.

When the escadrille arrived at Luxeuil it found a great surprise in the form of a large British aviation contingent. This detachment from the Royal Navy Flying Corps numbered more than fifty pilots and a thousand men. New hangars harboured their fleet of bombardment machines. Their own antiaircraft batteries were in emplacements near the field. Though detached from the British forces and under French command this unit followed the rule of His Majesty's armies in France by receiving all of its food and supplies from England. It had its own transport service.

Our escadrille had been in Luxeuil during the months of April and May. We had made many friends amongst the townspeople and the French pilots stationed there, so the older members of the American unit were welcomed with open arms and their new comrades made to feel at home in the quaint Vosges town. It wasn't long, however, before the Americans and the British got together. At first there was a feeling of reserve on both sides but once acquainted they became fast friends. The naval pilots were quite representative of the United Kingdom hailing as they did from England, Canada, New South Wales, South Africa, and other parts of the Empire. Most of them were soldiers by profession. All were officers, but they were as democratic as it is possible to be. As a result there was a continuous exchange of dinners. In a few days every one in this Anglo-American alliance was calling each other by some nickname and swearing lifelong friendship.

"We didn't know what you Yanks would be like," remarked one of the Englishmen one day. "Thought you might be snobby on account of being volunteers, but I swear you're a bloody human lot." That, I will explain, is a very fine compliment.

There was trouble getting new airplanes for every one in the escadrille. Only five arrived. They were the new model Nieuport fighting machine. Instead of having only 140 square feet of supporting surface, they had 160, and the forty-seven shot Lewis machine gun had been replaced by the Vickers, which fires five hundred rounds. This gun is mounted on the hood and by means of a timing gear shoots through the propeller. The 160 foot Nieuport mounts at a terrific rate, rising to 7,000 feet in six minutes. It will go to 20,000 feet handled by a skilful pilot.

It was some time before these airplanes arrived and every one was idle. There was nothing to do but loaf around the hotel, where the American pilots were quartered, visit the British in their barracks at the field, or go walking. It was about as much like war as a Bryan lecture. While I was in the hospital I received a letter written at this time from one of the boys. I opened it expecting to read of an air combat. It informed me that Thaw had caught a trout three feet long, and that Lufbery had picked two baskets of mushrooms.

Day after day the British planes practised formation flying. The regularity with which the squadron's machines would leave the ground was remarkable. The twenty Sopwiths took the air at precise intervals, flew together in a V formation while executing difficult manoeuvres, and landed one after the other with the exactness of clockwork. The French pilots flew the Farman and Breguet bombardment machines whenever the weather permitted. Every one knew some big bombardment was ahead but when it would be made or what place was to be attacked was a secret.

Considering the number of machines that were continually roaring above the field at Luxeuil it is remarkable that only two fatal accidents occurred. One was when a British pilot tried diving at a target, for machine-gun practice, and was unable to redress his airplane. Both he and his gunner were killed. In the second accident I lost a good friend—a young Frenchman. He took up his gunner in a two-seated Nieuport. A young Canadian pilot accompanied by a French officer followed in a Sopwith. When at about a thousand feet they began to manoeuvre about one another. In making a turn too close the tips of their wings touched. The Nieuport turned downward, its wings folded, and it fell like a stone. The Sopwith fluttered a second or two, then its wings buckled and it dropped in the wake of the Nieuport. The two men in each of the planes were killed outright.

Next to falling in flames a drop in a wrecked machine is the worst death an aviator can meet. I know of no sound more horrible than that made by an airplane crashing to earth. Breathless one has watched the uncontrolled apparatus tumble through the air. The agony felt by the pilot and passenger seems to transmit itself to you. You are helpless to avert the certain death. You cannot even turn your eyes away at the moment of impact. In the dull, grinding crash there is the sound of breaking bones.

Luxeuil was an excellent place to observe the difference that exists between the French, English, and American aviator, but when all is said and done there is but little difference. The Frenchman is the most natural pilot and the most adroit. Flying comes easier to him than to an Englishman or American, but once accustomed to an airplane and the air they all accomplish the same amount of work. A Frenchman goes about it with a little more dash than the others, and puts on a few extra frills, but the Englishman calmly carries out his mission and obtains the same results. An American is a combination of the two, but neither better nor worse. Though there is a large number of expert German airmen I do not believe the average Teuton makes as good a flier as a Frenchman, Englishman, or American.

In spite of their bombardment of open towns and the use of explosive bullets in their aerial machine guns, the Boches have shown up in a better light in aviation than in any other arm. A few of the Hun pilots have evinced certain elements of honour and decency. I remember one chap that was the right sort.

He was a young man but a pilot of long standing. An old infantry captain stationed near his aviation field at Etain, east of Verdun, prevailed upon this German pilot to take him on a flight. There was a new machine to test out and he told the captain to climb aboard. Foolishly he crossed the trench lines and, actuated by a desire to give his passenger an interesting trip, proceeded to fly over the French aviation headquarters. Unfortunately for him he encountered three French fighting planes which promptly opened fire. The German pilot was wounded in the leg and the gasoline tank of his airplane was pierced. Under him was an aviation field. He decided to land. The machine was captured before the Germans had time to burn it up. Explosive bullets were discovered in the machine gun. A French officer turned to the German captain and informed him that he would probably be shot for using explosive bullets. The captain did not understand.

"Don't shoot him," said the pilot, using excellent French, "if you're going to shoot any one take me. The captain has nothing to do with the bullets. He doesn't even know how to work a machine gun. It's his first trip in an airplane."

"Well, if you'll give us some good information, we won't shoot you," said the French officer.

"Information," replied the German, "I can't give you any. I come from Etain, and you know where that is as well as I do."

"No, you must give us some worth-while information, or I'm afraid you'll be shot," insisted the Frenchman.

"If I give you worth-while information," answered the pilot, "you'll go over and kill a lot of soldiers, and if I don't you'll only kill one—so go ahead."

The last time I heard of the Boche he was being well taken care of.

Kiffin Rockwell and Lufbery were the first to get their new machines ready and on the 23rd of September went out for the first flight since the escadrille had arrived at Luxeuil. They became separated in the air but each flew on alone, which was a dangerous thing to do in the Alsace sector. There is but little fighting in the trenches there, but great air activity. Due to the British and French squadrons at Luxeuil, and the threat their presence implied, the Germans had to oppose them by a large fleet of fighting machines. I believe there were more than forty Fokkers alone in the camps of Colmar and Habsheim. Observation machines protected by two or three fighting planes would venture far into our lines. It is something the Germans dare not do on any other part of the front. They had a special trick that consisted in sending a large, slow observation machine into our lines to invite attack. When a French plane would dive after it, two Fokkers, that had been hovering high overhead, would drop on the tail of the Frenchman and he stood but small chance if caught in the trap.

Just before Kiffin Rockwell reached the lines he spied a German machine under him flying at 11,000 feet. I can imagine the satisfaction he felt in at last catching an enemy plane in our lines. Rockwell had fought more combats than the rest of us put together, and had shot down many German machines that had fallen in their lines, but this was the first time he had had an opportunity of bringing down a Boche in our territory.

A captain, the commandant of an Alsatian village, watched the aerial battle through his field glasses. He said that Rockwell approached so close to the enemy that he thought there would be a collision. The German craft, which carried two machine guns, had opened a rapid fire when Rockwell started his dive. He plunged through the stream of lead and only when very close to his enemy did he begin shooting. For a second it looked as though the German was falling, so the captain said, but then he saw the French machine turn rapidly nose down, the wings of one side broke off and fluttered in the wake of the airplane, which hurtled earthward in a rapid drop. It crashed into the ground in a small field—a field of flowers—a few hundred yards back of the trenches. It was not more than two and a half miles from the spot where Rockwell, in the month of May, brought down his first enemy machine. The Germans immediately opened up on the wreck with artillery fire. In spite of the bursting shrapnel, gunners from a near-by battery rushed out and recovered poor Rockwell's broken body. There was a hideous wound in his breast where an explosive bullet had torn through. A surgeon who examined the body, testified that if it had been an ordinary bullet Rockwell would have had an even chance of landing with only a bad wound. As it was he was killed the instant the unlawful missile exploded.

Lufbery engaged a German craft but before he could get to close range two Fokkers swooped down from behind and filled his aeroplane full of holes. Exhausting his ammunition he landed at Fontaine, an aviation field near the lines. There he learned of Rockwell's death and was told that two other French machines had been brought down within the hour. He ordered his gasoline tank filled, procured a full band of cartridges and soared up into the air to avenge his comrade. He sped up and down the lines, and made a wide detour to Habsheim where the Germans have an aviation field, but all to no avail. Not a Boche was in the air.

The news of Rockwell's death was telephoned to the escadrille. The captain, lieutenant, and a couple of men jumped in a staff car and hastened to where he had fallen. On their return the American pilots were convened in a room of the hotel and the news was broken to them. With tears in his eyes the captain said: "The best and bravest of us all is no more."

No greater blow could have befallen the escadrille. Kiffin was its soul. He was loved and looked up to by not only every man in our flying corps but by every one who knew him. Kiffin was imbued with the spirit of the cause for which he fought and gave his heart and soul to the performance of his duty. He said: "I pay my part for Lafayette and Rochambeau," and he gave the fullest measure. The old flame of chivalry burned brightly in this boy's fine and sensitive being. With his death France lost one of her most valuable pilots. When he was over the lines the Germans did not pass—and he was over them most of the time. He brought down four enemy planes that were credited to him officially, and Lieutenant de Laage, who was his fighting partner, says he is convinced that Rockwell accounted for many others which fell too far within the German lines to be observed. Rockwell had been given the Médaille Militaire and the Croix de Guerre, on the ribbon of which he wore four palms, representing the four magnificent citations he had received in the order of the army. As a further reward for his excellent work he had been proposed for promotion from the grade of sergeant to that of second lieutenant. Unfortunately the official order did not arrive until a few days following his death.

The night before Rockwell was killed he had stated that if he were brought down he would like to be buried where he fell. It was impossible, however, to place him in a grave so near the trenches. His body was draped in a French flag and brought back to Luxeuil. He was given a funeral worthy of a general. His brother, Paul, who had fought in the Legion with him, and who had been rendered unfit for service by a wound, was granted permission to attend the obsequies. Pilots from all near-by camps flew over to render homage to Rockwell's remains. Every Frenchman in the aviation at Luxeuil marched behind the bier. The British pilots, followed by a detachment of five hundred of their men, were in line, and a battalion of French troops brought up the rear. As the slow moving procession of blue and khaki-clad men passed from the church to the graveyard, airplanes circled at a feeble height above and showered down myriads of flowers.

Rockwell's death urged the rest of the men to greater action, and the few who had machines were constantly after the Boches. Prince brought one down. Lufbery, the most skilful and successful fighter in the escadrille, would venture far into the enemy's lines and spiral down over a German aviation camp, daring the pilots to venture forth. One day he stirred them up, but as he was short of fuel he had to make for home before they took to the air. Prince was out in search of a combat at this time. He got it. He ran into the crowd Lufbery had aroused. Bullets cut into his machine and one exploding on the front edge of a lower wing broke it. Another shattered a supporting mast. It was a miracle that the machine did not give way. As badly battered as it was Prince succeeded in bringing it back from over Mulhouse, where the fight occurred, to his field at Luxeuil.

The same day that Prince was so nearly brought down Lufbery missed death by a very small margin. He had taken on more gasoline and made another sortie. When over the lines again he encountered a German with whom he had a fighting acquaintance. That is he and the Boche, who was an excellent pilot, had tried to kill each other on one or two occasions before. Each was too good for the other. Lufbery manoeuvred for position but, before he could shoot, the Teuton would evade him by a clever turn. They kept after one another, the Boche retreating into his lines. When they were nearing Habsheim, Lufbery glanced back and saw French shrapnel bursting over the trenches. It meant a German plane was over French territory and it was his duty to drive it off. Swooping down near his adversary he waved good-bye, the enemy pilot did likewise, and Lufbery whirred off to chase the other representative of Kultur. He caught up with him and dove to the attack, but he was surprised by a German he had not seen. Before he could escape three bullets entered his motor, two passed through the fur-lined combination he wore, another ripped open one of his woollen flying boots, his airplane was riddled from wing tip to wing tip, and other bullets cut the elevating plane. Had he not been an exceptional aviator he never would have brought safely to earth so badly damaged a machine. It was so thoroughly shot up that it was junked as being beyond repairs. Fortunately Lufbery was over French territory or his forced descent would have resulted in his being made prisoner.

I know of only one other airplane that was safely landed after receiving as heavy punishment as did Lufbery's. It was a two-place Nieuport piloted by a young Frenchman named Fontaine with whom I trained. He and his gunner attacked a German over the Bois le Pretre who dove rapidly far into his lines. Fontaine followed and in turn was attacked by three other Boches. He dropped to escape, they plunged after him forcing him lower. He looked and saw a German aviation field under him. He was by this time only 2,000 feet above the ground. Fontaine saw the mechanics rush out to grasp him, thinking he would land. The attacking airplanes had stopped shooting. Fontaine pulled on full power and headed for the lines. The German planes dropped down on him and again opened fire. They were on his level, behind and on his sides. Bullets whistled by him in streams. The rapid-fire gun on Fontaine's machine had jammed and he was helpless. His gunner fell forward on him, dead. The trenches were just ahead, but as he was slanting downward to gain speed he had lost a good deal of height, and was at only six hundred feet when he crossed the lines, from which he received a ground fire. The Germans gave up the chase and Fontaine landed with his dead gunner. His wings were so full of holes that they barely supported the machine in the air.

The uncertain wait at Luxeuil finally came to an end on the 12th of October. The afternoon of that day the British did not say: "Come on Yanks, let's call off the war and have tea," as was their wont, for the bombardment of Oberndorf was on. The British and French machines had been prepared. Just before climbing into their airplanes the pilots were given their orders. The English in their single-seated Sopwiths, which carried four bombs each, were the first to leave. The big French Brequets and Farmans then soared aloft with their tons of explosive destined for the Mauser works. The fighting machines, which were to convoy them as far as the Rhine, rapidly gained their height and circled above their charges. Four of the battle planes were from the American escadrille. They were piloted respectively by Lieutenant de Laage, Lufbery, Norman Prince, and Masson.

The Germans were taken by surprise and as a result few of their machines were in the air. The bombardment fleet was attacked, however, and six of its planes shot down, some of them falling in flames. Baron, the famous French night bombardier, lost his life in one of the Farmans. Two Germans were brought down by machines they attacked and the four pilots from the American escadrille accounted for one each. Lieutenant de Laage shot down his Boche as it was attacking another French machine and Masson did likewise. Explaining it afterward he said: "All of a sudden I saw a Boche come in between me and a Breguet I was following. I just began to shoot, and darned if he didn't fall."

As the fuel capacity of a Nieuport allows but little more than two hours in the air the *avions de chasse* were forced to return to their own lines to take on more gasoline, while the bombardment planes continued on into Germany. The

Sopwiths arrived first at Oberndorf. Dropping low over the Mauser works they discharged their bombs and headed homeward. All arrived, save one, whose pilot lost his way and came to earth in Switzerland. When the big machines got to Oberndorf they saw only flames and smoke where once the rifle factory stood. They unloaded their explosives on the burning mass.

The Nieuports having refilled their tanks went up to clear the air of Germans that might be hovering in wait for the returning raiders. Prince found one and promptly shot it down. Lufbery came upon three. He drove for one, making it drop below the others, then forcing a second to descend, attacked the one remaining above. The combat was short and at the end of it the German tumbled to earth. This made the fifth enemy machine which was officially credited to Lufbery. When a pilot has accounted for five Boches he is mentioned by name in the official communication, and is spoken of as an "Ace," which in French aerial slang means a super-pilot. Papers are allowed to call an "ace" by name, print his picture and give him a write-up. The successful aviator becomes a national hero. When Lufbery worked into this category the French papers made him a head liner. The American "Ace," with his string of medals, then came in for the ennuis of a matinee idol. The choicest bit in the collection was a letter from Wallingford, Conn., his home town, thanking him for putting it on the map.

Darkness was coming rapidly on but Prince and Lufbery remained in the air to protect the bombardment fleet. Just at nightfall Lufbery made for a small aviation field near the lines, known as Corcieux. Slow-moving machines, with great planing capacity, can be landed in the dark, but to try and feel for the ground in a Nieuport, which comes down at about a hundred miles an hour, is to court disaster. Ten minutes after Lufbery landed Prince decided to make for the field. He spi-ralled down through the night air and skimmed rapidly over the trees bordering the Corcieux field. In the dark he did not see a high-tension electric cable that was stretched just above the tree tops. The landing gear of his airplane struck it. The machine snapped forward and hit the ground on its nose. It turned over and over. The belt holding Prince broke and he was thrown far from the wrecked plane. Both of his legs were broken and he naturally suffered internal injuries. In spite of the terrific shock and his intense pain Prince did not lose consciousness. He even kept his presence of mind and gave orders to the men who had run to pick him up. Hearing the hum of a motor, and realizing a machine was in the air, Prince told them to light gasoline fires on the field. "You don't want another fellow to come down and break himself up the way I've done," he said.

Lufbery went with Prince to the hospital in Gerardmer. As the ambulance rolled along Prince sang to keep up his spirits. He spoke of getting well soon and returning to service. It was like Norman. He was always energetic about his flying. Even when he passed through the harrowing experience of having a wing shattered, the first thing he did on landing was to busy himself about getting another fitted in place and the next morning he was in the air again.

No one thought that Prince was mortally injured but the next day he went into a coma. A blood clot had formed on his brain. Captain Haff in command of the aviation groups of Luxeuil, accompanied by our officers, hastened to Gerardmer. Prince lying unconscious on his bed, was named a second lieutenant and decorated with the Legion of Honour. He already held the Médaille Militaire and Croix de Guerre. Norman Prince died on the 15th of October. He was brought back to Luxeuil and given a funeral similar to Rockwell's. It was hard to realize that poor old Norman had gone. He was the founder of the American escadrille and every one in it had come to rely on him. He never let his own spirits drop, and was always on hand with encouragement for the others. I do not think Prince minded going. He wanted to do his part before being killed, and he had more than done it. He had, day after day, freed the line of Germans, making it impossible for them to do their work, and three of them he had shot to earth.

Two days after Prince's death the escadrille received orders to leave for the Somme. The night before the departure the British gave the American pilots a farewell banquet and toasted them as their "Guardian Angels." They keenly appreciated the fact that four men from the American escadrille had brought down four Germans, and had cleared the way for their squadron returning from Oberndorf. When the train pulled out the next day the station platform was packed by khaki-clad pilots waving good-bye to their friends the "Yanks."

The escadrille passed through Paris on its way to the Somme front. The few members who had machines flew from Luxeuil to their new post. At Paris the pilots were reinforced by three other American boys who had completed their training. They were: Fred Prince, who ten months before had come over from Boston to serve in aviation with his brother Norman; Willis Haviland, of Chicago, who left the American Ambulance for the life of a birdman, and Bob Soubrian, of New York, who had been transferred from the Foreign Legion to the flying corps after being wounded in the Champagne offensive.

Before its arrival in the Somme the escadrille had always been quartered in towns and the life of the pilots was all that could be desired in the way of comforts. We had, as a result, come to believe that we would wage only a *de-luxe* war, and were unprepared for any other sort of campaign. The introduction to the Somme was a rude awakening. Instead of being quartered in a villa or hotel, the pilots were directed to a portable barracks newly erected in a sea of mud.

It was set in a cluster of similar barns nine miles from the nearest town. A sieve was a watertight compartment in comparison with that elongated shed. The damp cold penetrated through every crack, chilling one to the bone. There were no blankets and until they were procured the pilots had to curl up in their flying clothes. There were no arrangements for cooking and the Americans depended on the other escadrilles for food. Eight fighting units were located at the same field and our ever-generous French comrades saw to it that no one went hungry. The thick mist, for which the Somme is famous, hung like a pall over the birdmen's nest dampening both the clothes and spirits of the men.

Something had to be done, so Thaw and Masson, who is our *Chef de Popote* (President of the Mess) obtained permission to go to Paris in one of our light trucks. They returned with cooking utensils, a stove, and other necessary things. All hands set to work and as a result life was made bearable. In fact I was surprised to find the quarters as good as they were when I rejoined the escadrille a couple of weeks after its arrival in the Somme. Outside of the cold, mud, and dampness it wasn't so bad. The barracks had been partitioned off into little rooms leaving a large space for a dining hall. The stove is set up there and all animate life from the lion cub to the pilots centre around its warming glow.

The eight escadrilles of fighting machines form a rather interesting colony. The large canvas hangars are surrounded by the house tents of their respective escadrilles; wooden barracks for the men and pilots are in close proximity, and sandwiched in between the encampments of the various units are the tents where the commanding officers hold forth. In addition there is a bath house where one may go and freeze while a tiny stream of hot water trickles down one's shivering form. Another shack houses the power plant which generates electric light for the tents and barracks, and in one very popular canvas is located the community bar, the profits from which go to the Red Cross.

We had never before been grouped with as many other fighting escadrilles, nor at a field so near the front. We sensed the war to better advantage than at Luxeuil or Bar-le-Duc. When there is activity on the lines the rumble of heavy artillery reaches us in a heavy volume of sound. From the field one can see the line of sausage-shaped observation balloons, which delineate the front, and beyond them the high-flying airplanes, darting like swallows in the shrapnel puffs of anti-air-craft fire. The roar of motors that are being tested, is punctuated by the staccato barking of machine guns, and at intervals the hollow whistling sound of a fast plane diving to earth is added to this symphony of war notes.

Letters From Sergeant McConnell —At The Front

We're still waiting for our machines. In the meantime the Boches sail gaily over and drop bombs. One of our drivers has been killed and five wounded so far but we'll put a stop to it soon. The machines have left and are due to-day.

You ask me what my work will be and how my machine is armed. First of all I mount an *avion de chasse* and am supposed to shoot down Boches or keep them away from over our lines. I do not do observation, or regulating of artillery fire. These are handled by escadrilles equipped with bigger machines. I mount at daybreak over the lines; stay at from 11,000 to 15,000 feet and wait for the sight of an enemy plane. It may be a bombardment machine, a regulator of fire, an observer, or an *avion de chasse* looking for me. Whatever she is I make for her and manoeuvre for position. All the machines carry different gun positions and one seeks the blind side. Having obtained the proper position one turns down or up, whichever the case may be, and, when within fifty yards, opens up with the machine gun. That is on the upper plane and it is sighted by a series of holes and cross webs. As one is passing at a terrific rate there is not time for many shots, so, unless wounded or one's machine is injured by the first try—for the enemy plane shoots, too—one tries it again and again until there's nothing doing or the other fellow is dropped. Apart from work over the lines, which is comparatively calm, there is the job of convoying bombardment machines. That is the rotten task. The captain has called on us to act as guards on the next trip. You see we are like torpedo boats of the air with our swift machines.

We have the honour of being attached to a bombardment squadron that is the most famous in the French Army. The captain of the unit once lost his whole escadrille, and on the last trip eight lost their lives. It was a wonderful fight. The squadron was attacked by thirty-three Boches. Two French planes crashed to earth—then two German; another German was set on fire and streaked down, followed by a streaming column of smoke. Another Frenchman fell; another German; and then a French lieutenant, mortally wounded and realizing that he was dying, plunged his airplane into a German below him and both fell to earth like stones.

The tours of Alsace and the Vosges that we have made, to look over possible landing places, were wonderful. I've never seen such ravishing sights, and in regarding the beauty of the country I have missed noting the landing places. The valleys are marvellous. On each side the mountain slopes are a solid mass of giant pines and down these avenues of green tumble myriads of glittering cascades which form into sparkling streams beneath. It is a pleasant feeling to go into Alsace and realize that one is touring over country we have taken from the Germans. It's a treat to go by auto that way. In the air, you know, one feels detached from all below. It's a different world, that has no particular meaning, and besides, it all looks flat and of a weary pattern.

THE FIRST TRIP

Well, I've made my first trip over the lines and proved a few things to myself. First, I can stand high altitudes. I had never been higher than 7,000 feet before, nor had I flown more than an hour. On my trip to Germany I went to 14,000 feet and was in the air for two hours. I wore the fur head-to-foot combination they give one and paper gloves under the fur ones you sent me. I was not cold. In a way it seemed amusing to be going out knowing as little as I do. My *mitrailleuse* had been mounted the night before. I had never fired it, nor did I know the country at all even though I'd motored along our lines. I followed the others or I surely should have been lost. I shall have to make special trips to study the land and be able to make it out from my map which I carry on board. For one thing the weather was hazy and clouds obscured the view.

We left en escadrille, at 30-second intervals, at 6:30 A.M. I'd been on guard since three, waiting for an enemy plane. I climbed to 3,500 feet in four minutes and so started off higher than the rest. I lost them immediately but took a compass course in the direction we were headed. Clouds were below me and I could see the earth only in spots. Ahead was a great barrier of clouds and fog. It seemed like a limitless ocean. To the south the Alps jutted up through the clouds and glistened like icebergs in the morning sun. I began to feel completely lost. I was at 7,000 feet and that was all I knew. Suddenly I saw a little black speck pop out of a cloud to my left—then two others. They were our machines and from then on I never let them get out of my sight. I went to 14,000 in order to be able to keep them well in view below me. We went over Belfort which I recognized, and, turning, went toward the lines. The clouds had dispersed by this time. Alsace was below us and in the distance I could see the straight course of the Rhine. It looked very small. I looked down and saw the trenches and when I next looked for our machines I saw clusters of smoke puffs. We were being fired at. One machine just under me seemed to be in the centre of a lot of shrapnel. The puffs were white, or black, or green, depending on the size of the shell used. It struck me as more amusing than anything else to watch the explosions and smoke. I thought of what a lot of money we were making the Germans spend. It is not often that they hit. The day before one of our machines had a part of the tail shot away and the propeller nicked, but that's just bum luck. Two shells went off just at my height and in a way that led me to think that the third one would get me; but it didn't. It's hard even for the aviator to tell how far off they are. We went over Mulhouse and to the north. Then we sailed south and turned over the lines on the way home. I was very tired after the flight but it was because I was not used to it and it was a strain on me keeping a look-out for the others.

At Verdun

To-day the army moving picture outfit took pictures of us. We had a big show. Thirty bombardment planes went off like clock-work and we followed. We circled and swooped down by the camera. We were taken in groups, then individually, in flying togs, and God knows what-all. They will be shown in the States.

If you happen to see them you will recognize my machine by the MAC, painted on the side.

Seems quite an important thing to have one's own airplane with two mechanics to take care of it, to help one dress for flights, and to obey orders. A pilot of no matter what grade is like an officer in any other arm.

We didn't see any Boche planes on our trip. We were too many. The only way to do is to sneak up on them.

I do not get a chance to see much of the biggest battle in the world which is being fought here, for I'm on a fighting machine and the sky is my province. We fly so high that ground details are lacking. Where the battle has raged there is a broad, browned band. It is a great strip of murdered Nature. Trees, houses, and even roads have been blasted completely away. The shell holes are so numerous that they blend into one another and cannot be separately seen. It looks as if shells fell by the thousand every second. There are spurts of smoke at nearly every foot of the brown areas and a thick pall of mist covers it all. There are but holes where the trenches ran, and when one thinks of the poor devils crouching in their inadequate shelters under such a hurricane of flying metal, it increases one's respect for the staying powers of modern man. It's terrible to watch, and I feel sad every time I look down. The only shooting we hear is the tut-tut-tut of our own or enemy plane's machine guns when fighting is at close quarters. The Germans shoot explosive bullets from theirs. I must admit that they have an excellent air fleet even if they do not fight decently.

I'm a sergeant now—*sergent* in French—and I get about two francs more a day and wear a gold band on my cap, which makes old territorials think I'm an officer and occasions salutes which are some bother.

A SORTIE

We made a foolish sortie this morning. Only five of us went, the others remaining in bed thinking the weather was too bad. It was. When at only 3,000 feet we hit a solid layer of clouds, and when we had passed through, we couldn't see anything but a shimmering field of white. Above were the bright sun and the blue sky, but how we were in regard to the earth no one knew. Fortunately the clouds had a big hole in them at one point and the whole mass was moving toward the lines. By circling, climbing, and dropping we stayed above the hole, and, when over the trenches, worked into it, ready to fall on the Boches. It's a stunt they use, too. We finally found ourselves 20 kilometres in the German lines. In coming back I steered by compass and then when I thought I was near the field I dived and found myself not so far off, having the field in view. In the clouds it shakes terribly and one feels as if one were in a canoe on a rough sea.

Victor Chapman

I was mighty sorry to see old Victor Chapman go. He was one of the finest men I've ever known. He was *too* brave if anything. He was exceptionally well educated, had a fine brain, and a heart as big as a house. Why, on the day of his fatal trip, he had put oranges in his machine to take to Balsley who was lying wounded with an explosive bullet. He was going to land near the hospital after the sortie.

Received letter inclosing note from Chapman's father. I'm glad you wrote him. I feel sure that some of my letters never reach you. I never let more than a week go by without writing. Maybe I do not get all yours, either.

A Smash-Up

Weather has been fine and we've been doing a lot of work. Our Lieutenant de Laage de Mieux, brought down a Boche. I had another beautiful smash-up. Prince and I had stayed too long over the lines. Important day as an attack was going on. It was getting dark and we could see the tiny balls of fire the infantry light to show the low-flying observation machines their new positions. On my return, when I was over another aviation field, my motor broke. I made for field. In the darkness I couldn't judge my distance well, and went too far. At the edge of the field there were trees, and beyond, a deep cut where a road ran. I was skimming ground at a hundred miles an hour and heading for the trees. I saw soldiers running to be in at the finish and I thought to myself that James's hash was cooked, but I went between two trees and ended up head on against the opposite bank of the road. My motor took the shock and my belt held me. As my tail went up it was cut in two by some very low 'phone wires. I wasn't even bruised. Took dinner with the officers there who gave me a car to go home in afterward.

To-day I shared another chap's machine (Hill of Peekskill), and got it shot up for him. De Laage (our lieutenant) and I made a sortie at noon. When over the German lines, near *Côte* 304, I saw two Boches under me. I picked out the rear chap and dived. Fired a few shots and then tried to get under his tail and hit him from there. I missed, and bobbed up alongside of him. Fine for the Boche, but rotten for me! I could see his gunner working the *mitrailleuse* for fair, and felt his bullets darn close. I dived, for I could not shoot from that position, and beat it. He kept plunking away and altogether put seven holes in my machine. One was only ten inches in from me. De Laage was too far off to get to the Boche and ruin him while I was amusing him.

Yesterday I motored up to an aviation camp to see a Boche machine that had been forced to land and was captured. On the way up I passed a cantonment of Senegalese. About twenty of 'em jumped up from the bench they were sitting on and gave me the hell of a salute. Thought I was a general because I was riding in a car, I guess. They're the blackest niggers you ever saw. Good-looking soldiers. Can't stand shelling but they're good on the cold steel end of the game. The Boche machine was a beauty. Its motor is excellent and she carries a machine gun aft and one forward. Same kind of a machine I attacked to-day. The German pilots must be mighty cold-footed, for if the Frenchmen had airplanes like that they surely would raise the devil with the Boches.

As it is the Boches keep well within their lines, save occasionally, and we have to go over and fight them there.

KIFFIN ROCKWELL

Poor Kiffin Rockwell has been killed. He was known and admired far and wide, and he was accorded extraordinary honours. Fifty English pilots and eight hundred aviation men from the British unit in the Vosges marched at his funeral.

There was a regiment of Territorials and a battalion of Colonial troops in addition to the hundreds of French pilots and aviation men. Captain Thénault of the American Escadrille delivered an exceptionally eulogistic funeral oration. He spoke at length of Rockwell's ideals and his magnificent work. He told of his combats. "When Rockwell was on the lines," he said, "no German passed, but on the contrary was forced to seek a refuge on the ground."

Rockwell made the *esprit* of the escadrille, and the Captain voiced the sentiments of us all when, in announcing his death, he said: "The best and bravest of us all is no more."

How does the war look to you—as regards duration? We are figuring on about ten more months, but then it may be ten more years. Of late things are much brighter and one can feel a certain elation in the air. Victory, before, was a sort of academic certainty; now, it's felt.

CHAPTER 4

How France Trains Pilot Aviators

France now has thousands of men training to become military aviators, and the flying schools, of which there is a very great number, are turning out pilots at an astounding rate.

The process of training a man to be a pilot aviator naturally varies in accordance with the type of machine on which he takes his first instruction, and so the methods of the various schools depend on the apparatus upon which they teach an *élève pilote*—as an embryonic aviator is called—to fly.

In the case of the larger biplanes, a student goes up in a dual-control airplane, accompanied by an old pilot, who, after first taking him on many short trips, then allows him part, and later full, control, and who immediately corrects any false moves made by him. After that, short, straight line flights are made alone in a smaller-powered machine by the student, and, following that, the training goes on by degrees to the point where a certain mastery of the apparatus is attained. Then follows the prescribed "stunts" and voyages necessary to obtain the military brevet.

TRAINING FOR PURSUIT AIRPLANES

The method of training a pilot for a small, fast *avion de chasse,* as a fighting airplane is termed, is quite different, and as it is the most thorough and interesting I will take that course up in greater detail.

The man who trains for one of these machines never has the advantage of going first into the air in a double-control airplane. He is alone when he first leaves the earth, and so the training preparatory to that stage is very carefully planned to teach a man the habit of control in such a way that all the essential movements will come naturally when he first finds himself face to face with the new problems the air has set for him. In this preparatory training a great deal of weeding out is effected, for a man's aptitude for the work shows up, and unless he is by nature especially well fitted he is transferred to the division which teaches one to fly the larger and safer machines.

First of all, the student is put on what is called a roller. It is a low-powered machine with very small wings. It is strongly built to stand the rough wear it gets, and no matter how much one might try it could not leave the ground. The apparatus is jokingly and universally known as a Penguin, both because of its humorous resemblance to the quaint arctic birds and its inability in common with them to do any flying. A student makes a few trips up and down the field in a double-control Penguin, and learns how to steer with his feet. Then he gets into a single-seated one and, while the rapidly whirling propeller is pulling him along, tries to keep the Penguin in a straight line. The slightest mistake or delayed movement will send the machine skidding off to the right or left, and sometimes, if the motor is not stopped in time, over on its side or back. Something is always being broken on a Penguin, and so a reserve flock is kept at the side of the field in order that no time may be lost.

After one is able to keep a fairly straight line, he is put on a Penguin that moves at a faster rate, and after being able to handle it successfully passes to a very speedy one, known as the "rapid." Here one learns to keep the tail of the machine at a proper angle by means of the elevating lever, and to make a perfectly straight line. When this has been accomplished and the monitor is thoroughly convinced that the student is absolutely certain of making no mistakes in guiding with his feet, the young aviator is passed on to the class which teaches him how to leave the ground. As one passes from one machine to another one finds that the foot movements must be made smaller and smaller. The increased speed makes the machine more and more responsive to the rudder, and as a result the foot movements become so gentle when one gets into the air that they must come instinctively.

First Flights Alone

The class where one will leave the ground has now been reached, and an outfit of leather clothes and *casque* is given to the would-be pilot. The machines used at this stage are low-powered monoplanes of the Blériot type, which, though being capable of leaving the ground, cannot rise more than a few feet. They do not run when the wind is blowing or when there are any movements of air from the ground, for though a great deal of balancing is done by correcting with the rudder, the student knows nothing of maintaining the lateral stability, and if caught in the air by a bad movement would be apt to sustain a severe accident. He has now only to learn how to take the machine off the ground and hold it at a low line of flight for a few moments.

For the first time one is strapped into the seat of the machine, and this continues to be the case from this point on. The motor is started, and one begins to roll swiftly along the ground. The tail is brought to an angle slightly above a straight line. Then one sits tight and waits. Suddenly the motion seems softer, the motor does not roar so loudly, and the ground is slipping away. The class standing at the end of the line looks far below; the individuals are very small, but though you imagine you are going too high, you must not push to go down more than the smallest fraction, or the machine will dive and smash. The small push has brought you down with a bump from a seemingly great height. In reality you have been but three feet off the ground. Little by little the student becomes accustomed to leaving the ground, for these short hop-skip-and-jump flights, and has learned how to steer in the air.

If he has no bad smash-ups he is passed on to a class where he rises higher, and is taught the rudiments of landing. If, after a few days, that act is reasonably performed and the young pilot does not land too hard, he is passed to the class where he goes about sixty feet high, maintains his line of flight for five or six minutes and learns to make a good landing from that height. He must by this time be able to keep his machine on the line of flight without dipping and rising, and the landings must be uniformly good. The instructor takes a great deal of time showing the student the proper line of descent, for the landings must be perfect before he can pass on.

Now comes the class where the pilot rises three or four hundred feet high and travels for more than two miles in a straight line. Here he is taught how to combat air movements and maintain lateral stability. All the flying up to this point has been done in a straight line, but now comes the class where one is taught to turn. Machines in this division are almost as high powered as a regular flying machine, and can easily climb to two thousand feet. The turn is at first very wide, and then, as the student becomes more confident, it is done more quickly, and while the machine leans at an angle that would frighten one if the training in turning had not been gradual. When the pilot can make reasonably close right and left turns, he is told to make figure eights. After doing this well he is sent to the real flying machines.

There is nothing in the way of a radical step from the turns and figure eights to the real flying machines. It is a question of becoming at ease in the better and faster airplanes taking greater altitudes, making little trips, perfecting landings, and mastering all the movements of correction that one is forced to make. Finally one is taught how to shut off and start one's motor again in the air, and then to go to a certain height, shut off the motor, make a half-turn while dropping and start the motor again. After this, one climbs to about two thousand feet and, shutting off the motor, spirals down to within five hundred feet of the ground. When that has been practised sufficiently, a registering altitude meter is strapped to the pilot's back and he essays the official spiral, in which one must spiral all the way to earth with the motor off, and come to a stop within a few yards of a fixed point on the aviation grounds. After this, the student passes to the voyage machines, which are of almost twice the power of the machine used for the short trips and spirals.

Tests for the Military Brevet

There are three voyages to make. Two consist in going to designated towns an hour or so distant and returning. The third voyage is a triangle. A landing is made at one point and the other two points are only necessary to cross. In addition, there are two altitudes of about seven thousand feet each that one has to attain either while on the voyages or afterward.

The young pilot has not, up to this point, had any experience on trips, and there is always a sense of adventure in starting out over unknown country with only a roller map to guide one and the gauges and controls, which need constant attention, to distract one from the reading of the chart. Then, too, it is the first time that the student has flown free and at a great height over the earth, and his sense of exultation at navigating at will the boundless sky causes him to imagine he is a real pilot. True it is that when the voyages and altitudes are over, and his examinations in aeronautical sciences passed, the student becomes officially a *pilote-aviateur,* and he can wear two little gold-woven wings on his collar to designate his capacity, and carry a winged propeller emblem on his arm, but he is not ready for the difficult work of the front, and before he has time to enjoy more than a few days' rest he is sent to a school of *perfectionnement.* There the real, serious and thorough training begins.

Schools where the pilots are trained on the modern machines—*écoles de perfectionnement* as they are called—are usually an annex to the centres where the soldiers are taught to fly, though there are one or two camps that are devoted exclusively to giving advanced instruction to aviators who are to fly the *avions de chasse,* or fighting machines. When the aviator enters one of these schools he is a breveted pilot, and he is allowed a little more freedom than he enjoyed during the time he was learning to fly.

He now takes up the Morane monoplane. It is interesting to note that the German Fokker is practically a copy of this machine. After flying for a while on a low-powered Morane and having mastered the landing, the pilot is put on a new, higher-powered model of the same make. He has a good many hours of flying, but his trips are very short, for the whole idea is to familiarize one with the method of landing. The Blériot has a landing gear that is elastic in action, and it is easy to bring to earth. The Nieuport and other makes of small, fast machines for which the pilot is training have a solid wheel base, and good landings are much more difficult to make. The Morane pilot has the same practices climbing to small altitudes around eight thousand feet and picking his landing from that height with motor off. When he becomes proficient in flying the single- and double-plane types he leaves the school for another, where shooting with machine guns is taught.

This course in shooting familiarizes one with various makes of machine guns used on airplanes, and one learns to shoot at targets from the air. After two or three weeks the pilot is sent to another school of combat.

TRICK FLYING AND DOING STUNTS

These schools of combat are connected with the *écoles de perfectionnement* with which the pilot has finished. In the combat school he learns battle tactics, how to fight singly and in fleet formation, and how to extract himself from a too dangerous position. Trips are made in squadron formation and sham battles are effected with other escadrilles, as the smallest unit of an aerial fleet is called. For the first time the pilot is allowed to do fancy flying. He is taught how to loop the loop, slide on his wings or tail, go into corkscrews and, more important, to get out of them, and is encouraged to try new stunts.

Finally the pilot is considered well enough trained to be sent to the reserve, where he waits his call to the front. At the reserve he flies to keep his hand in, practises on any new make of machine that happens to come out or that he may be put on in place of the Nieuport, and receives information regarding old and new makes of enemy airplanes.

At last the pilot receives his call to the front, where he takes his place in some established or newly formed escadrille. He is given a new machine from the nearest airplane reserve centre, and he then begins his active service in the war, which, if he survives the course, is the best school of them all.

CHAPTER 5

Against Odds

Since the publication of previous editions of "Flying for France" we have obtained the following letters which add greatly to the interest and complete the record of McConnell's connection with the Lafayette Escadrille.

March 19, 1917.
Dear Paul

We are passing through some very interesting times. The Boches are in full retreat, offering very little resistance to the English and French advance. The Boches have systematically destroyed all the towns and villages abandoned. Where they haven't burned a house, they have made holes through the roofs with pickaxes. All the cross-roads are blown up at the junctions, and when the trees bordering the roads haven't been cut down, barricading the roads, they have been cut half way through so that when the wind blows they keep falling on the passing convoys. The inhabitants left in these villages are wild with delight and are giving the troops an inspiring reception. In one town the Boches raped all the women before leaving, then locked them down cellar, and carried off all the young girls with them.

We have been flying low, and watching the cavalry overrunning the country. The Boches are retreating to very strongly fortified positions, where the advance is going to come up against a stone wall.

This morning Genet and McConnell flew well ahead of the advancing army, Mac leading. Genet saw two Boche planes manoeuvring to get above them, so he began to climb, too. Finally they got together; the Boche was a biplane and had the edge on Genet. Almost the first shot got Genet in the cheek. Fortunately it was only a deep flesh wound, and another shot almost broke the stanchion, which supports the wings, in two. Genet stuck to the Boche and opened fire on him. He knows he hit the machine and at one time he thought he saw the machine on fire, but nothing happened. At last the Boche had Genet in a bad position, so he (Genet) piqued down about a thousand meters and got away from the Boche. He looked around for Mac but couldn't find him, so he came home. Mac hasn't yet shown up and we are frightfully worried. Genet has a dim recollection that when he attacked the Boche, the other Boche piqued down in Mac's direction, and it looks as if the Boche got Mac unawares. Late this afternoon we got a report that this morning a Nieuport was seen to land near Tergnier, which is unfortunately still in German hands. This must have been Mac's, in which case he is only wounded, or perhaps only his machine was badly damaged. There is a general feeling among us that Mac is all right. The French cavalry are within ten or fifteen kilometres of Tergnier now and perhaps they will take the place to-morrow, in which case we will certainly learn something. This afternoon Lieut. de Laage and Lufbery landed at Ham, where the advance infantry were, and made a lot of inquiries. It was near this place where the fight started. Nobody had seen any machine come down. You may be sure I will keep you informed of everything that turns up. Genet is going to write you in a day or so.

Sincerely,

Walter Lovell

P. S. I apologize for the mistakes and the disconnectedness of this letter, but I wrote it in frightful haste in order to get it in the first post.

March 20, 1917.

My Dear Rockwell

I do not know if any of the boys have written you about the disappearance of Jim, so perhaps you might know something about it when this letter reaches you.

He left yesterday at 8:45 a.m. in his machine for the German lines, and has not returned yet. He and Genet were attacked by two Germans, the latter, who received a slight wound on the cheek, was so occupied he did not see what became of Jim, and returned without him.

The combat took place between Ham and St. Quentin; the territory was still occupied by the enemy when the combat took place. The worst I hope has happened to our friend is that perhaps he was wounded and was forced to land in the enemy's lines and was made prisoner. Nothing definite is known. I shall write you immediately I get news.

I am extremely worried. To lose my friend would be a severe blow. I can't and will not believe that anything serious has happened.

Best wishes,

Sincerely,

E. A. Marshall

Escadrille N. 124

Secteur Postal 182

March 21, 1917

My Dear Paul

Had I been feeling less distressed and miserable on Monday morning, or during yesterday, I would have written you then, but I told Lovell to tell you how I felt when he wrote on Monday and that I would try and write in a day or so. I am not feeling much better mentally but I'll try and write something, for I am the only one who was out with poor Mac on Monday morning and it just adds that much more to my distress.

As you know, we have had a big advance here, due to the

deliberate evacuation by the Germans, without much opposition, of the territory now in the hands of the French and English. The advance began last Thursday night and each day has brought the lines closer to Saint Quentin and the region north and south of it.

On Monday morning Mac, Parsons, and myself went out at nine o'clock on the third patrol of the escadrille. We had orders to protect observation machines along the new lines around the region of Ham. Mac was leader. I came second and Parsons followed me. Before we had gone very far Parsons was forced to go back on account of motor trouble, which handicapped us greatly on account of what followed, but of course that cannot be remedied because Parsons was perfectly right in returning when his motor was not running well. We all do that one time or another.

Mac and I kept on and up to ten o'clock were circling around the region of Ham, watching out for the heavier machines doing reconnoitring work below us. We went higher than a thousand meters during that time. About ten, for some reason or other of his own, Mac suddenly headed into the German lines toward Saint Quentin and I naturally followed close to his rear and above him. Perhaps he wanted to make observations around Saint Quentin. At any rate, we had gotten north of Ham and quite inside the hostile lines, when I saw two Boche machines crossing towards us from the region of Saint Quentin at an altitude quite higher than ours. We were then about 1,600 meters. I supposed Mac saw them the same as I did. One Boche was much farther ahead than the other, and was headed as if he would dive at any moment on Mac. I glanced ahead at Mac and saw what direction he was taking, and then pulled back to climb up as quickly as possible to gain an advantageous height over the nearest Boche. It was cloudy and misty and I had to keep my eyes on him all the time, so naturally I couldn't watch Mac. The second Boche was still much farther off than his mate. By this time I had gotten to 2,200, the Boche was almost up to me and taking a diagonal course right in front. He started to circle and his gunner—it was a biplane, probably an Albatross, although the mist was too thick and dark for me to see much but the bare outline of his dirty, dark green body, with white and black crosses—opened fire before I did and his first volley did some damage. One bullet cut the left central support of my upper wing in half, an explosive bullet cut in half the left guiding rod of the left aileron, and I was momentarily stunned by part of it which dug a nasty gouge into my left cheek. I had already opened fire and was driving straight for the Boche with teeth set and my hand gripping the triggers making a veritable stream of fire spitting out of my gun at him, as I had incendiary bullets, it being my job lately to chase after observation balloons, and on Saturday morning I had also been up after the reported Zeppelins. I had to keep turning toward the Boche every second, as he was circling around towards me and I was on the inside of the circle, so his gunner had all the advantage over me. I thought I had him on fire for one instant as I saw—or supposed I did—flames on his fuselage. Everything passed in a few seconds and we swung past each other in opposite directions at scarcely twenty-five meters from each other—the Boche beating off towards the north and I immediately dived down in the opposite direction wondering every second whether the broken wing support would hold together or not and feeling weak and stunned from the hole in my face. A battery opened a heavy fire on me as I went down, the shells breaking just behind me. I straightened out over Ham at a thousand meters, and began to circle around to look for Mac or the other Boche, but saw absolutely nothing the entire fifteen minutes I stayed there. I was fearful every minute that my whole top wing would come off, and I thought that possibly Mac had gotten around toward the west over our lines, missed me, and was already on his way back to camp. So I finally turned back for our camp, having to fly very low and against a strong northern wind, on account of low clouds just forming. I got back at a quarter to eleven and my first question to my mechanic was: "Has McConnell returned?"

He hadn't, Paul, and no news of any sort have we had of him yet, although we hoped and prayed every hour yesterday for some word to come in. The one hope that we have is that on account of this continued advance some news will be brought in of Mac through civilians who might have witnessed his flight over the lines north of Ham, while they were still in the hands of the enemy, for many of the civilians in the villages around there are being left by the Germans as they retire. We can likewise hope that Mac was merely forced to land inside the enemy lines on account of a badly damaged machine, or a bad wound, and is well but a prisoner. I wish to God, Paul, that I had been able to see Mac during his combat, or had been able to get down to him sooner and help him. The mists were thick, and consequently seeing far was difficult. I would have gone out that afternoon to look for him but my machine was so damaged it took until yesterday afternoon to be repaired. Lieut. de Laage and Lufbery did go out with their Spads and looked all around the region north of Ham towards Saint Quentin but saw nothing at all of a Nieuport on the ground, or anything else to give news of what had occurred.

The French are still not far enough towards Saint Quentin to be on the territory where the chances are Mac landed, so we'll still have to wait for to-day's developments for any possibility of news. I got lots of hope, Paul, that Mac is at least alive although undoubtedly a prisoner. I know how badly the news has affected you. We're all feeling mighty blue over it and as for myself—I'm feeling utterly miserable over the whole affair. Just as soon as any definite news comes in I'll surely let you know at once. Meanwhile, keep cheered and hopeful. There's no use in losing hope yet. If a prisoner Mac may even be able to escape and return to our lines, on account of the very unsettled state of the retreating Germans. Others have done so under much less favourable conditions.

I hope you are having a very enjoyable trip through the South. Walter showed me the postal you wrote him, which he received yesterday. Please give my very warm regards to your wife. Write as soon as you can, too.

Very faithfully yours,

Edmond C. C. Genet

March 22, 1917

My Dear Rockwell

Still no news about Jim. Last night the captain sent out a request to the military authorities to have our troops advancing in the direction of Saint Quentin report immediately any particulars about avion 2055. Even now I cannot reconcile myself concerning Jim's fate. I hope he has been made prisoner.

Just a few words about myself. I am awaiting the results of my friends' actions in the States on my behalf. I am placed in a peculiar position in the escadrille. I have nothing to do here. Shall I take care of Jim's belongings?

Best wishes,

Sincerely,

E. A. Marshall

Escadrille N. 124

Secteur Postal 182

March 23, 1917

Dear Paul

In my letter I promised to send you word as soon as any definite news came in concerning poor Mac. To-day word came in from a group of French cavalry that they witnessed our fight on Monday morning and that they saw Mac brought down inside the German lines towards Saint Quentin after being attacked by two Boche machines and at the same time they saw me fighting a third one higher than Mac, and that just as I piqued down Mac fell so there were three Boche machines instead of two, as I supposed, having missed seeing the third one on account of the heavy clouds and mist around us.

There is still the hope that Mac wasn't killed but only wounded and a prisoner. If he is we'll learn of it later. The cavalrymen didn't say whether he came down normally or fell. Possibly he was too far off really to tell definitely about that. Certainly he had been already brought down before I could get down to help him after the Boche I attacked beat it off. Had I known there were three Boche machines I certainly would not have played around that Boche at such a distance from Mac.

When will Mrs. Weeks return to Paris from the States? Will you write and tell her about Mac? She'll be mighty well grieved to hear of it, I know, and you'll be the best one to break it to her.

Write to me soon. Best regards to Mrs. Rockwell.

E. Genet

March 24th, a. m.
C. Aeronautique
Noyon & D. C. 13
My Dear Rockwell

The targe element informs us that it has found, in the environs of the Bois l'Abbe, a Nieuport No. 2055. The aviator, a sergeant, has been dead since three days, in the opinion of the doctor. His pockets appear to have been searched, for no papers were found on him. The Bois l'Abbe is two kilometres south of Jussy. The above message received by us at ten o'clock last night. Jussy is on the main road between Saint Quentin and Chauny. I expect to go back to the infantry soon.

Sincerely,

E. A. Marshall

Escadrille N. 124
Secteur Postal 182
March 25, 1917
Dear Paul

The evening before last definite news was brought to us that a badly smashed Nieuport had been found by French troops, beside which was the body of a sergeant-pilot which had been there at least three days and had been stripped of all identification papers, flying clothes and even the boots. They got the number of the machine, which proved without further question that it was poor Mac. They gave the location as being at the little village of Petit Detroit, which is just south of Flavy-le-Martel, the latter place being about ten kilometres east of Ham on the railroad running from Ham to La Fere.

After having made a flight over the lines yesterday morning, I went down around Petit Detroit to locate the machine. There was no decent place there on which to land so I circled around over it for a few minutes to see in which condition it (the Nieuport) was. The machine was scarcely distinguishable so badly had it smashed into the ground, and there is scarcely any doubt, Paul, that Mac was killed while having his fight in the air, as no pilot would have attempted to land a machine in the tiny rotten field—no more than a little orchard beside the road—voluntarily. It seems almost certain that he struck the ground with full motor on. Captain Thénault landed some distance from there that he might go over there in a car and see just what could be done about poor Mac's body. When he returned last night he told us the following:

Mac, he said, was as badly mangled as the machine and had been relieved of his flying suit by the damned Boches, also of his shoes and all papers. The machine had struck the ground so hard that it was half buried, the motor being totally in the earth and the rest, including even the machine gun, completely smashed. It was just beside the main road, in a small field containing apple trees cut down by the retreating Boches, and just at the southern edge of the village.

Mac has been buried right there beside the road, and we will see that the grave is decently marked with a cross, etc. The captain brought back a square piece of canvas cut from one of the wings, and we are going to get a good picture we have of Mac enlarged and placed on this with a frame. I suppose that Thaw or Johnson will attend to the belongings of Mac which he had written are to be sent to you to care for. In the letter which he had left for just such an occasion as this he concludes with the following words: "Good luck to the rest of you. God damn Germany and vive la France!"

All honour to him, Paul. The world will look up to him, as well as France, for whom he died so gloriously, just as it is looking up to your fine brother and the rest of us who have given their lives so freely and gladly for this big cause.

Warmest regards, etc.,

Faithfully,

Edmond C. C. Genet

P. S. The captain has already put in a proposal for a citation for Mac, and also one for me. Mac surely deserved it, and lots more too.

Escadrille N. 124
S. P. 182
March 27, 1917
Dear Paul

I got your postcard to-day and would have written you sooner about poor Jim but haven't been up to it, which I know you understand.

It hit me pretty hard, Paul, for as you know we were in school and college together, and for the last four or five years have been very intimate, living in N.C. and New York together.

It's hell, Paul, that all the good boys are being picked off. The damned Huns have raised hell with the old crowd, but I think we have given them more than we have received.

The boys who have gone made the name for the escadrille and now it's up to us who are left (especially the old Verdun crowd) to keep her going and make the Boches suffer.

Like old Kiffin, Mac died gloriously and in full action. It was in a fight with three Germans in their lines. Genet took one Hun (and was wounded). The last he saw was a Hun on Mac's back. Later we learned from the cavalry that there were two on Mac and after a desperate fight Mac crashed to the ground. This was the 19th of March. Three days later we took the territory Mac fell in and they were unable to distinguish who he was. The swine Huns had taken every paper or piece of identification from him and also robbed him—even took his shoes. The captain went over and was able to identify him by the number of his machine and uniform. He had lain out there three days and was smashed so terribly that you couldn't recognize his face. He was buried where he fell in a coffin made from the door of a pillaged house. His last resting place (and where he fell) is "Petit Detroit," which is a village southwest of Saint Quentin and north of Chauney. He is buried just at the southeast end of the village and in a hell of a small town.

Jim left a letter of which I am copying the important parts:

In case of my death or made prisoner—which is worse—please send my canteen and what money I have on me, or coming to me (he had none on him as the Huns lifted that) to Mr. Paul A. Rockwell, 80 rue, etc. Shoes, tools, wearing apparel, etc., you can give away. The rest of my things, such as diary, photos, souvenirs, *croix de guerre*, best uniform (he had best uniform on and I think the *croix de guerre*—however, you may find the latter in his things, his other uniform can't be found), please put in canteen and ship along.

Kindly cable my sister, Mrs. Followsbee, 65 Bellevue Place, Chicago. It would be kind to follow same by a letter telling about my death (which I am doing).

I have a box trunk in Paris containing belongings I would like to send home. Paul R. knows about it and can attend to the shipping. I would appreciate it if the committee of the American Escad. would pay to Mr. Paul Rockwell the money needed to cover express.

My burial is of no import. Make it as easy as possible for yourselves. I have no religion and do not care for any service. If the omission would embarrass you I presume I could stand the performance.

Good luck to the rest of you. God damn Germany and *vive la France.*

J. R. McConnell

Note Jim's keen sense of humour even to death instructions.

Jim had on the day of his death been proposed for the Croix de Guerre with palm. When it comes I shall send it to you.

Well, Paul, I have told you everything I can think of, but if there are any omissions or questions don't hesitate to ask.

I think we are now beginning to see the beginning of the end. The devastation, destruction and misery the Huns have left is a disgraceful crime to civilization and is pitiful. It drives me so furious I can't talk about it.

Best regards to you, old boy, and luck. All join in the above. I shall wind up the same as Jim.

As always,

Chout

Charles Chouteau Johnson

P. S. Steve Biglow is taking canteen to your place in Paris to-morrow, so you will find it there upon your return.

C. C. J.

Our Pilots in the Air

by William B. Perry

CHAPTER 1

A Bombing Air Raid

The scene in the valley was striking in one respect. Low ranges of gently sloping hills had widened out, enclosing broad levels with what in America would be termed a creek but was here poetically named a river. By here I mean eastern France, not so many miles from No-Man's-Land. The "striking" feature was the "Flying Camp" spread out over a dead level of much trampled greensward, enclosed by high board walls, irregularly oval in shape, with a large clump of trees in the centre and a multiplicity of large, small, mostly queer-shaped buildings scattered about.

There were a few wide roadways, with smaller avenues intersecting them, and larger open spaces, bordered by hangars, at either end of the oval.

On a bulletin board in one of these open spaces a placard was tacked, at which several young men in khaki and wearing the aviator cap were gazing, commenting humorously or otherwise. All that this plainly open placard published, apparently for all eyes to see, was as follows:

Members of Bombing Squadron No. — will be on the *qui vive* at 7 p.m. tonight. Specific orders will be issued to each at that time.

Not much in that, an outsider might think. But wait! Listen!

"Say, Orry," remarked an athletic youth, throwing an arm casually over the shoulder of a smaller companion beside him and tweaking the other's ear, "does this mean that you and me go up together in that crazy old biplane they foisted on us before?"

"How should I know?" replied the smaller lad, a nervous, sprightly youngster, dark-eyed, curly-headed, thin-faced. "Did she get your nerve last time?"

"Not by a long shot! But when we made that last dive to get away from Fritzy in his Fokker, I noticed your hands on the crank were shaking. Say, if that Tommy in the monoplane hadn't helped us, where'd we been?"

"Right here, you goose! We'd have got out somehow, but it was squally for about five minutes."

The two strolled off together as others, also in khaki but with different fittings or insignia, gathered about to read, comment and then turn their several ways.

"We are in that bombing squad all right, I guess remarked Lafe Blaine, the athletic youngster. "But I am tired of this everlasting bombing that goes on, mostly by night. We're chums, Orry; we work together all right. There is no one in this camp can handle a fighting machine better than I; nor do I want a better, truer backer at the Lewis than you."

The Lewis gun was the one then most in use at this aerodrome station, which was somewhere on that section near where the British and French sectors meet.

"You always were a bully boy, Lafe, in spite of your two big handles. Say, how'd they come to call you Lafayette when you already had such a whopper of a surname?"

"Oh, dry up, Orry! Those names often make me tired. I'm only an ordinary chap, but with those names every noodle thinks I ought to be something real big. Catch on?"

Orris Erwin nodded and pinched the other's massive forearm, as he replied:

"So you are big! Bet you weigh one-eighty if you weigh a pound."

But Lafe was thinking. Finally he announced decidedly:

"I'm going to get after our Sergeant this afternoon. If he

knows what's what, he'll let you and me take out that neat little Bleriot. We'll do our share of bombing of course; but if the
Boches come up after us, we can do something else besides
run for home—eh?"

Erwin shook his head dubiously as he replied:

"I doubt if he gives us the Bleriot. It's French, you know.
We're practicing with the Tommies. He likes the way you
handle things, but I fear he don't build much on me."

Lafe, of course, disclaimed any superiority, but Orris felt
that way. Later, when mid-day chow was over, Lafe found
his way to where the squadron commander was checking off
the different machines and assigning to each the various occupants. All this on a pad, in one of the hangars, with no one
else near, as the Sergeant thought. In Hangar Four were two
Bleriots all in trim order. The Sergeant stared at one of them,
grumbling to himself.

"What will I do here?" he reflected, half aloud, though
unconscious of his words. "I forgot that Cheval's arm is giving
him trouble. Confound him! He's too risky. Won't do to leave
one of these behind. Hm-m-m! Who else —"

"Your pardon, Sergeant!" A tall, athletic young American
was beside him, standing respectfully attention. "Why not
take me? Give me a chance!"

So dominating, yet so deferential was Blaine's attitude and
manner that Sergeant Anson for the minute said nothing, but
he stared at the lad.

"I was with Monsieur Cheval, Sir, the night he got hurt, and
I brought the machine home, under his direction of course.
You ask him if I am not competent to handle that Bleriot. I'd
much rather be in it than in the big biplane I used last time."

"But—but—you're too young, too inexperienced, too—
too—"

"Now, Sir, please ask Cheval! You know what his judg-
ment is. If I am to have an observer, let Cheval go. He can sit,
and—and observe—"

"Dash your bally impertinence!" Anson was putting up a

tremendous bluff. He knew it, and he knew that Blaine probably knew it, but "What do you know about Bleriots, anyway?" he asked.

In five minutes by enticing talk and really export fingering of the various parts of the admirable mechanism, Blaine half convinced his superior. More, for by adroit manipulation of a certain lock, with wrench and a pair of tweezers, he readjusted a certain valve hinge in the petrol tank which he had heard Monsieur Cheval grumbling about before. This he did with such dexterous rapidity and ease that Anson expressed approval, adding:

"Where did you pick up so much mechanical knowledge, Blaine?"

"At Mineola, in the States. They kept every applicant in the shops—some of them for weeks, others permanently."

"How happened it they didn't keep you there?" Anson was grinning now.

"Well, Sir, I wanted to learn to fly—high. That's what I went into aviation for. Before that I worked for the Wrights at Dayton. Well, when I tried flying, it happened there was a prize offered for flying to Manhattan and back, going round the Liberty Statue. I got hold of an old Curtis machine and somehow I came back second in the race. But —" here Blaine grinned at his own recollection, "but I pretty near busted up that old Curtis! After that they kept me flying until I finally came over here."

The Sergeant frowned then smiled and jotted something down on his pad.

"Go and see Monsieur Cheval. If he is not well enough to go with you—well, have you anyone else in view?"

"Yes, sir. My partner, who has gone with me on several raids. He's all right —"

"If you were disabled or killed, could he bring this machine back?"

"Yes, sir. He is as good as I am. Cool as a cucumber, but he—he's rather modest. In fact, if I don't get Cheval, I must have him, with your permission of course."

"Or without it, eh?" Anson again smiled, this time genially. "Well, well! Do what I have said. If you have to do without Cheval, bring that youngster who is so modest to me. I will judge." And the Sergeant turned off, resuming his pencilling and further wandering as if Blaine were not there.

Half an hour later Lafe stood by the cot where a shallow-faced, trim-moustached man lay groaning discontentedly. At sight of the young American he raised up to a sitting position, disclosing his right arm and wrist still in splints and bandages. Moreover the pains of moving himself made him groan and ejaculate after the mercurial manner or the Frenchman un-used to lying still and eager always to be up and doing.

"Ah, it ees *mon* comrade Blaine! Ver welcome—mooch so! Wish mooch you speak ze language, ze French."

Monsieur Cheval, really a noted aviator, had chummed much with the American contingent and had been in the States once, though only for a short time. But he had learned "ze language"—after a fashion. When Blaine briefly explained what he wanted and what the squadron commander had said, Cheval lay back with a deep sigh, saying:

"*Merci*, comrade!" Here he chuckled. "I like to go: I want to go! But I no use to you now. Not at all! I no use to myself. Voila! I got well queek; better so here; not over yon in No-Man's-Land. But you be sure bring my enfant back safe, my Bleriot—Ah! A great baby is my Bleriot!"

Blaine promised to do his best. His pal and comrade, Orris Erwin, was also good, safe—in short, reliable.

"Never fear, Monsieur Cheval! Unless they get us up yon-der," pointing vaguely upward into the sky, "we will fetch her back all right. Good luck! Try to be out as soon as you can. We miss you on these little trips after Fritzy."

An hour later Blaine, accompanied by Erwin, stood before Sergeant Anson in the latter's cubby-hole of an office, while a stream of khaki-clad young men filed in one by one. Anson waved them aside until the others had left, then turned to Blaine.

"I saw Cheval myself," said the Sergeant grimly. "He wanted to go but it will be a week before he can use that arm, aside from other injuries. I spoke to Captain Byers about you. He was reluctant, but owing to the newness of so many of you Yankee airmen, he was unable to make suggestions. Only this- you two must be careful, cautious —"

"Not too cautious, I hope, sir!" came promptly from Blaine, while Orris smiled behind his sleeve. "A pilot has to risk things, you know."

"Don't interrupt!" Anson ordered sharply, though his eyes twinkled. "You know what I mean. Can you bring the plane back, Erwin, if anything happens to Blaine?"

"Yes, sir, I think so. I've often flown before, alone —"

"Under fire?" This sharp reply from the Sergeant.

"I was in the last raid after Vimy Ridge, Sir. Brenzer, the pilot, was killed. I managed to get back to our lines."

"You been over some time?"

"Yes, Sir. Only part of the time I was stationed at Aldershot, as assistant trainer for a bunch of raw rookies from our side."

One long look at both Anson gave, then turned away with:

"You'll do. Both of you be on hand for chow at regular time. Then await instructions." He waved them off.

CHAPTER 2

The Whir of Wings

Shortly after a bugle call the following order was posted in the general mess hall for all concerned to read.

Members of Bombing Squadron No. — will carry out the following order. 10 a.m., 12 midnight, 2 a.m. are the respective times to start. At each time three machines, each carrying eight 25 pound bombs, will bomb respectively R———, C———, L———. Secrecy is imperative. Each member of the three squads thus assigned will be ready at Hangars No. —, No. —, No. — at times mentioned above.

Meantime each aviator, with his observer, had been privately notified by the Sergeant in person. This was an everyday operation order and was taken as a matter of course. These night raids are mostly for the purpose of keeping the Boche busy and nervous after hard days and nights in the front trenches, thus supposedly lowering his morale. Usually the points thus selected are the shell-torn villages back of the front, where Fritz has been sent for a brief period of rest before being sent to the front again. About the time he lies down in the half-ruined house that is his billet, and dreams of home and conquering peace, a bomb falls inside. The walls are further shattered, some of his comrades killed or maimed, he perhaps among them. Other bombs fall, heavy explosions result, and Fritz finds that his night's rest is lost in general turmoil. This continues night after night and the damage to German morale is enormous.

From the point of view of the air-service, things are different. These night raids are a matter of course with the pilots. It is part of the regular work.

When Blaine and Erwin climbed into the Bleriot, bombs already stowed, and it was wheeled out in front of the hangar, everything was very quiet. A minute later they were climbing up into the inky darkness at the appointed signal, the only noises being the whirrings of their own and two other two machines appointed for the two A. M. hour.

Watching for the signal of the leader of the squad, at the right time they headed for the further front.

Over the trenches star-shells from the infantry could be seen. Under direction they headed over No-Man's-Land, keeping at sufficient altitude, hugging the darkness, avoiding glints of light, dodging occasional searchlights, and all practically without a word spoken.

"You've been out here before, Lafe"' said Orris at last. "How much further are we going?"

"Be there in two minutes. Keep easy! I'm going lower. Get your bombs ready."

Silently Erwin obeyed. Below lay blackness, relieved at one point by a few dots of light that marked the ruins of the hamlet on which they were to let loose the bombs. So far no sign of life in the air or below appeared.

The three machines in this detachment had scattered in order to distribute their supply of bombs at a given signal from the leader. In this night raid an escorting fleet that usually accompanied the daytime raids was omitted. There was little need.

"Now!" cautioned Blaine to Orris and the latter began to drop his first sheaf, a rather heavy one as the bombs weighed twenty-five pounds each. Others were at work also and the village below, already in half ruins, began to detonate with sharp explosions, lurid flashings and an uproar of human cries. It was evident that the raiders had struck the right spot.

For some minutes the work went on, Blaine swooping still lower, until glimpses of hurried scurryings of the soldiers thus rudely disturbed were mingled with the larger glares from the continuous explosions.

Orris Erwin, through though smaller and slighter physically, worked away until the last sheaf was exhausted.

Then, and only then, the scene below was illuminated by the flash and roar of hostile artillery. A shell exploded with a deafening report so near their Bleriot that it was evident that the firer had sighted them during Lafe's last lower swoop.

On the instant Blaine pressed a trigger, elevating the sharp nose of the machine. As the deflected planes responded to sundry manipulations at certain levers and they began to climb spirally into the upper air, the powerful engines, exerting greater strength, shot them rapidly upward where height and obscurity lessened the danger of further shots.

"Well, Archie came near getting us then, eh?" This from Lafe.

Receiving no answer, he glanced aside. What was his dismay to see Erwin's slender figure drooping nervelessly, his head sinking, and the emptied sheaf of bombs sprawling neglected in his lap!

"You're hit, Orry? For God's sake buck up! I've still got to climb or they'll get us yet."

Clamping his knee round the wheel, he managed with one hand to pull Orris forward and sideways, so that the boy's curly head, now capless, lay against his thigh. With one arm half around and upon that senseless head, holding the slight frame from slipping, he still manipulated the alert Bleriot, that responded instantly to each human spur with a mobility that was almost life-like.

The two other machines had vanished in the darkness, doubtless cleaving the higher air strata in a backward flight to the home aerodrome, which was now the goal of all. Meantime searchlights were flashing here, there, yonder through the inky sky. The swift reports of anti-aircraft guns split the night's silence in a most disconcerting manner. Erwin groaned and twisted his body.

"Stay still, Orry! We must 'a' been the last to quit, and they're making things hot back westward."

Here a blinding gleam of light flashed athwart his eyes and, letting go of Erwin, he darted aside suddenly on a differing course. Erwin's body crumpled into a heap. A heavier man might have toppled over the edge, perhaps hanging helplessly at peril of falling out, unless held by the straps which many old aviators neglect. As it was, the nerveless lad was held by the high rim of the opening that fenced them both in. For the moment the boy was safe.

Giving his whole attention to the machine, Blaine zig-zagged and dodged, mounting ever and ever higher. Yet his trend was unavoidably towards the east, further within the enemy lines.

"For the present I've got to go this way," he thought. "I hope Lex and Milt got away west before those 'cussed Archies broke loose. We'll have to stay quiet until this ruction below settles down." Lex and Milt were the pilots of the two remaining machines of this, the third and last section of the bombing squadron of that night.

"Orry! Oh, Orry! Wakeup! Aren't you all right yet?"

These and other adjurations Blaine would make from time to time. A chill came over him more than once as he wondered if Erwin would not recover. Once only as Lafe moved his own leg, pressing it unduly hard against the other, Erwin gave another groan.

A whir as of wings sounded in his rear, and Blaine became aware of shadowy movements through the faintly growing light in the east. Undoubtedly it must be a hostile machine. He had been spotted as he flew eastward. In addition to the now waning fire from the Archies, planes were now out after him. Divining this, Blaine wheeled, put on more power and flow towards the northwest, the German keeping after him at increasing speed. As the light increased the clinging shadow in the east grew more plain. Whoever it was, the pursuer was determined not to be shaken off. Soon he would begin firing.

At this junction Erwin gave Blaine's leg an undeniable kick. He was at last reviving. The pilot leaned towards his bunkie.

"Say, Orry, are you coming to at last?"

Another kick, evidently part of a struggle by Orris to right himself.

Blaine saw the German making the first spiral upward, in an effort to attain a position suitable for using the machine gun. Blaine therefore zigzagged more to westward, thereby throwing the reviving Erwin into an easier position. At this an easier position. At this Blaine was pleased to see his friend look wonderingly at him and the bowed head slightly raise itself.

"Lay still right where you are, Orry," murmured Lafe. "There's a Boche after us. We've got out of Archie's range, but I've one of their planes on our heels. Whist! Git down lower! He's going to fire. If he does, I—I'll crumple up. We'll land and—and—"

Further talk ceased as the simultaneous rattle and spatter of opposing machine guns made talk impracticable. Blaine was below, the Boche above, each whirling, diving, spiralling as dexterous pilots do in such conflict.

True to his promise amid the first exchange of shots, watching both Erwin's recovery and the German, now closer than ever, Blaine concealed himself.

And now, seeing that Orris was quite revived, and following Blaine's counsel, they presented to the German only a collapsed form, half leaning as if hit again. Blaine, almost out of sight, steered groundward.

"Are you strong enough now to take my place?"

"I—I think so," returned the still reviving Erwin. "What you going to do—land?"

At this juncture the machine hit the ground in a decreasing glide, while Blaine, half rising, pitched forward as if dead.

"Take the machine, Orry," Blaine had said. "I'm dead; you're wounded."

Knowing that Blaine had his plans laid, Erwin followed. Then the Boche, feeling pretty good over the idea that he had captured an enemy machine with two men in it, also alighted from his own a few rods distant. To his view there appeared one man dead and another wounded.

Covering Erwin with his revolver as he sat leaning back ghastly and still bleeding from the shrapnel that had at first struck him down, the German eyed his apparently helpless victims.

"Get oudt!" he snapped in rather poor English to Erwin.

The latter started to obey, still covered by the pistol at his head. Suddenly Blaine, who had tumbled to the ground at the first landing, now sat up, his own revolver pointed straight at the German.

"Throw down that gun!" he announced in clear, steady tones. "Quick! No nonsense, Fritz!"

One brief stare. Then, realizing that he had been out-generaled, he sullenly obeyed. To his further amazement, Erwin, now quite recovered, rose up, got out, and though weak tied the Boche hard and fast under Blaine's direction.

"Now, Orry," said Lafe, looking his comrade over carefully, "are you right enough to take our machine back?"

"Bet your sweet life I am!" Orry's face was still pale, while blood was coagulated in his curly short hair. "I'm all right, Lafe. What are we going to do?"

"We'll put this chap in his own machine, and I'll take it and him back."

"You mean provided Fritzy lets us get through safe."

"Und zat ve wond do! Forshtay?" This from the now sullen German standing by bound hand and foot, yet mentally antagonistic still.

"Don't you worry, bo," said Blaine, coolly picking up the man, a follow of no small weight, and lifting, him into his own machine, a big Taube of many horse-power. "That is, if you've got petrol enough."

This was assured beyond doubt by subsequent examination. The German safely stowed, Erwin and Blaine made a hurried yet accurate inspection of both planes, and Orris at once started westward. Blaine was about to follow when horse hoofs were heard beyond a hedge not far away. The German's eyes flashed. He divined a forcible rescue. He began to yell, but with a swift move Blaine gagged him with his own bandanna 'kerchief.

The German struggled but Blaine had tied him also to the posts supporting the hollow chamber wherein pilot and observer sat, and now springing in himself, he started off.

Right then the heads of a column of cavalry debouched in the field. The roar of roar of the Taube filled the air and in an instant they saw what was happening. By this time Orris was well up in the air and still spiralling higher. The Taube, with which Blaine was already partly familiar through prior captured machines among the Allies, was making its first upward curve, when a thought came to Blaine. A ruse! The German lay still helpless, bound and gagged. Though struggling with his bonds, his eyes were spitting anger.

In its case, with pulley attached, was a small flag of one of the larger German aerial squadrons. Blaine plucked it forth, jerked the pulley cord, and there unrolled before all eyes the Imperial eagle, with certain other designs, all on a black background, and with a death's head in white at each corner. It was two or three feet square, and as it floated from one of the poles sustaining the biplanes, no one in the clear morning light could mistake its meaning.

Blaine himself was not sure as to the flag. But it really was the one used only by a certain squadron especially endorsed and. supported by the Kaiser and the Royal House of Hohenzollern and of which the Crown Prince was the special patron. By the time Blaine was above the treetops, some twenty or thirty horsemen had debouched into the sheep pasture where these happenings took place. They were lancers and, mistaking the real nature of this manoeuvre, every lance was depressed in salute and a horse shout rose up that sounded much like a series of Hochs with Kaiser at the end.

"Holy smoke!" said Blaine, getting the machine gun in shooting trim with one hand while manipulating the controls with the other. "Say, Fritzy," to the snarling German at his feet, who fairly writhed at his bounds and gag, "your folks think I'm off after those English or Yankee *schwein*! Savvy?"

But here a sudden change came over the scene.

Fighting Both Enemy
and Elements

The Bleriot which Erwin was now piloting, though far in the upper air, was seen to be whirling round and returning, apparently to Blaine's rescue.

Evidently Orris had also seen the irruption of lancers and had no intention of deserting his comrade and friend while in possible peril. To intensify the strain he began to spray the Germans below with the remaining sheaf of bullets in the magazine of the machine gun.

Seeing no further need of camouflage on the part of the Americans, Blaine, with one foot crushing down the German, who was now attempting to rise despite his bonds, whirled the German machine gun round upon the now suspicious lancers below.

These were unslinging their carbines. Blaine anticipated them with a spatter of bullets from their own weapon. At this bedlam broke loose below.

While Erwin had done little or no damage, probably owing to distance, Blaine's discharge was point-blank and deadly.

Meantime in some way the German managed to loosen one arm. Recklessly he seized hold of one the controls, wrenching it violently.

"You will, will you?" exclaimed the American, "We must get away from here at any rate!"

Releasing both hands, he seized the German by the throat,

pinning him against the rim of the hole that held both, and with his feet on the accelerator rose rapidly upward. By this time bullets were spitting round them, one of which seared the German's bare scalp deeply. Uttering a curious groan, the fellow sank back and Blaine released his throat.

"He's out of it for the time being," thought Lafe. "Good thing, too. Hard work to keep a strangle hold on that chap and keep his machine right side up. Hey there, Orry!"

By this time Erwin had forged so close in swinging round again that only a few yards separated the planes.

"Don't you go any nearer those Boches. I am all right. We got some of them. Look at those riderless horses!"

True it was that several riderless horses were careering about the field below. Also at another angle some men were dragging forth an antiaircraft gun, or so it looked to be by its peculiar carriage and mounting.

"Sure you are all right?" called Orris as the two machines sped along side by side, all the while rising. "Didn't that fellow give you trouble?"

"None to speak of. I've looped a cord about his throat, and got the other end round a cleat. If he tries to jerk away he'll strangle. Put on more power, man! Can't you see they've dragged the Archies out and are stuffing in sheaves of bullets?"

"All right!" called Erwin, now spiralling higher, higher, climbing cloudward. "Sure you got the Taube straight—hey, Lafe?"

"Course I have! Didn't I work one of them at —?" But the name was lost to Orris as the distance increased.

To Blaine's relief the Boche did not move for a moment or two. This gave him time to twist that free arm back where Lafe could press the weight of one big foot thereon, and also complete the adjustment of the cord. He arranged it by looping twice round the cleat, the length reaching to Fritz's throat being drawn taut. Moreover, as the German's body was resting sidewise upon his other arm, still tightly bound, Blaine felt that he had the man for the time being at least.

Now came heavier roars from below. Not only one gun but several had been brought up, trained on the fliers and were being fired rapidly at the receding airplanes.

Also the true nature of the situation aloft must have been divined. Hence the extreme activity among the Germans, now trying desperately to reverse the progress of events by bringing one or both machines down. The fact that the life of one of their own comrades might be snuffed out did not weigh with them at all. Such is the German militaristic creed. The individual, his life, or welfare is as nothing when compared with the welfare of the cause, the state, the whole brutal, efficient system.

After all, this comrade might be dead now. They must get at and, if possible, overtake these *schwein* at all cost. Were not they retreating with a choice Prussian machine, that even now flaunted in derision the Death's Head Flag?

No wonder the Boches were mad—good mad!

But our Yankee adventurers were by no means at the end of their raid. The sun was rising. With the rare promise of a clear day, considering the time and the region, it was more evident than usual that a very high altitude must be reached and maintained.

There were the German trenches to be passed, the trenches raided only a few hours before, the No-Man's-Land, before the welcoming shelter of friendly areas and support might be reached. At any rate, they could see and signal other and also keep close together and be ready to afford mutual support in case of meeting the foe. This last was soon verified by the rise and approach of a small squadron of scout cruisers, winged monoplanes, each with a ed monoplanes, each with a single pilot only and one machine gun.

"Keep well under them," signalled Blaine to his friend. "Got any ammunition? What? The devil!"

Orris had replied to Lafe's queries by shaking out the now empty cartridge sheaves and dropping them again. Lafe, then swooping closer, Called forth to his mate:

"By its looks this gun is a rebuilt Lewis. Can you use any of mine? You know the Boches are great in reconstructing captured weapons to their own use. Get below me and to one side. Hurry up! I'll try to toss you a sheaf. Here—damn you!"

This to the German who again evinced signs of life. Having no time to spare, Blaine jerked the throat cord closer and gave a heavier foot pressure to the prisoner's twisted arm. Meanwhile with no time to lose, Orris swooped lower, rising gently under Blaine's right or starboard side. The latter had to rise in order to toss the weighty sheaf of cartridges exactly where he wished them to fall—into Erwin's lap.

This he did successfully. But in so doing his weight relaxed upon the Boche's arm. At the same time Orris, in catching the sheaf, allowed his control grip to relax. The nose of Orris's machine, now rising, bumped into Lafe's under plane, tilting it up sharply.

Precisely at this juncture, and as Blaine's foot pressure on his prisoner's arm relaxed, the tilting planes threw him sharply forward, down and upon the German. The latter, seeing his one chance, wrenched his partially released arm forward and caught it round Blaine's legs as he stumbled. At the same time this double movement somehow operated to release Fritz's other arm.

By now, Orris, unconscious of the mischief his own upward shove had caused, sheered his machine aside, still climbing upward and onward, only to find three of the enemy scouts nearing rapidly and making ready for an encounter.

Looking back, he saw, in the place of Blaine's leather cap and goggles, a dimly shimmering twinkle of arms and legs flashing above the rim of the open enclosure where the pilots sit.

"Great guns!" he ejaculated, his blood tingling with thrills. "That chap has got loose and they're having it. What must I do?"

Even while these thoughts were flashing, he was working. He dared not turn to Blaine's relief. He did not know yet if the sheaf thrown him would fit his own machine gun. But first he must dip, circle, come up underneath and try his luck.

As has been said, Orry was no novice. He had flown at the front for months as one of the Lafayette Escadrille. Before that he had worked his way up in aerial mechanics in the United States and also here in France.

Even while diving, circling, swirling in mid air, ten thousand feet up, he was adjusting the new sheaf to his own gun. Happily it fitted.

That was a good sign, and pirouetting, not unlike an expert dancer executing a new turn, he dove aside and came up fairly behind the nearest Boche. Without hesitation he began to spray the enemy with a shower of their own bullets. It was indeed lucky the new cartridges fitted. It was merely one blunder committed by the extra efficient Germans in converting British weapons to their own use.

Evidently the ammunition dealt out to the Death's Head Squadron was of the best. It was intentionally so. Another proof of this lay in the fact that the German plane thus attacked fell sideways, recovered, plunged half staggering away, while a tiny spark of flame became visible to Erwin as he sheered aside in the opposite direction and prepared for a new onset from above by the second plane. So far as he could see, the other plane was making for Blaine's machine that still flow the Death's Head Flag. Yet it was acting strangely as seen from a distance by the Boches, who might or might not be posted as to the strange change of its ownership.

The second plane, rendered more cautious by the fate of the first, which was now descending a mass of flames, began a series of divings, wrigglings, and even nose dips, in its efforts to confuse Erwin and find a good position from which to shower the daring invader with bullets.

On his own part Orris went through the usual manoeuvres customary when two airmen, both skilful, are seeking the advantage of the other. Well it was for the young man that his own Bleriot was one of the best of the up-to-date fighting planes.

Numerous shots were taken on both sides, and in the excitement f or the moment Orris lost all sight of the fate of his partner. At last, in trying by a desperate and perilous manoeuvre, to "get on the tail" of his adversary by a side-loop in mid-flight, the Boche pilot, while upside down, came for an instant fairly within range. Quickly Orris took his advantage.

He was above and to the right of the German, and with a single whirl of his Lewis gun brought it fully in line with the Boche's head as he sat head down, strapped in his seat, while his machine was swiftly turning in its side evolution so as to bring him in the rear of his enemy.

"Now!" gasped Orris, beginning his bullet spray. "Help me, Mars!"

A queer prayer, but it was quickly answered. The German machine righted more slowly, however. Erwin dove swiftly down and came upright in the rear of his now swaying adversary. Then the lad saw what fate had done for him.

The German had collapsed in his seat, to which, as has been said, he had strapped himself. His head lay on the rim, apparently a mass of streaming crimson. His machine, a renovated Fokker, was tipsily zigzagging along without any guidance except its stabilizer and its own momentum.

To say the boy was half paralyzed at first is not too strong. But a revulsion swept through him in a flood. At the same time there came to his brain a vivid flash, reminding him that while thus desperately engaged for his own life, he had heard sounds of aerial battling somewhere in his rear.

While he was making up his mind what to do next, the whir of speeding motors rose rapidly. Looking back, he saw the Death's Head flag waving from the nearest one and soon distinguished Blaine, apparently all right, but chugging away at top speed in Erwin's direction.

Just now the Fokker with its dead occupant gave another side drop and, uninfluenced by the usual controls, came nearly to a standstill. It toppled again, then down it went earthward at increasing speed, carrying its occupant along.

"Hey-you!" This from Blaine as he swept up and by, while

rounding to. "Look behind! I dropped that chap—the first one! But he's brought a lot of others. Let's make for home, boy!"

Apparently it was too late without a further scrimmage, for no less than half a dozen Boche planes were swooping around their rear, some already within range. In manoeuvring into position Blaine again picked up his megaphone, saying:

"I saw you drop those chaps. Oh, you Orry! Here we go— right for some more of them! Whoopee!"

It seemed little short of blasphemy—this uproarious spirit, in the face of the odds gathering in behind. But Blaine was built that way. Danger, the closer and more menacing, instead of rousing fear, nerved him to his best or, as it might turn out, worst.

"Where's your prisoner?" shouted Erwin. "I feared he'd get you."

"Nit, old man! I got hold of a monkey-wrench and knocked him cold. But he was game, you bet!"

"Where is he then?"

"Cold and stiff under my feet. Watch out, Orry!"

Megaphones cast aside, both Americans now addressed themselves to the desperate task of fighting these new assailants and reaching their own lines.

But in the first firing that ensued Erwin's Lewis gun suddenly jammed. This was probably one result of his having to use the German-made ammunition tossed to him earlier by Blaine, when his own had been exhausted. He signalled to his partner:

"Gun jammed! Must cut for home—understand?"

"All right! Go up—up—"

A burst of flame from Blaine's machine, and the toppling down of the nearest adversary was the first result of this new encounter. Evidently that flag waving from Blaine's captured plane had fooled the Boches again.

Down, down went the hostile machine, its pilot frantically but ineffectually trying to right himself.

Passing Erwin, the latter saw the Boche, evidently a mere

lad, working at the controls as the plane dropped down like a dead leaf in the air.

"Poor fellow," sighed Orris, beginning to spiral upward. "What a deadly cruel thing war now is!"

Up, up he climbed, two of the enemy following, while Blaine was engaging another, the last. The final view Erwin had of his bunkie the two were engaged in a close duel, dipping, darting, flashing about each other. Now came interchanging machine gun fire, with both gradually following Erwin higher, higher, until the latter began to feel that the thin air of these upper regions was getting on his nerves. A glance at his own register showed eighteen thousand feet or thereabouts.

Still his adversaries climbed after him. Now and then a spurt of flame and a spatter of bullets indicated that his own plane was being more or less perforated. The lad became doubtful as to the wisdom of waiting longer for his comrade. Evidently Blaine would fight on as long as his ammunition lasted or until disabled himself. After all, two hostile planes dropped and the third one brought home with its occupant was not a bad conclusion for a night's bombing raid on the enemy trenches.

Here a sudden, fierce gust of wind from the north catching him unawares half tilted his machine and then as he righted it sent him scurrying at terrific speed southward. At the same time a black cloud, belching and flaming thunder and lightning, swept down on him with almost the force of a hurricane.

CHAPTER 4

Winning Promotions

Looking back, Orris saw his nearest foe, apparently caught by the same whirlwind that had nearly unseated him, go side-looping over and over as if in the grasp of mighty, invisible forces that he was unable to meet or control.

"It's safety first, I guess, for us all," he thought, at once diving into the nearing thunder burst that closed round him like a black pall, a pall now threaded and convulsed with electric forces that showed only in vivid flashes and deafening thunders.

The winds, too, picked him up, whirled him about and otherwise so tossed his machine here, there, yonder, that for five fearful minutes he hardly knew where or what he was. The wind, now bitter cold, would have frozen his flesh but for his sheathing of wool and leather that protected his face, arms and body. Blinding gusts of rain, sleet and frozen snow buffeted the planes, the shield of the fuselage, and all of himself that was visible.

By this time Blaine, the German planes, his own late adversary, had all vanished. He was alone, like a buffeted, tossed, shaken twig, in that wild vortex of darkness and storm.

With his machine gun jammed and his petrol running low, what was there for him to do but descend and make for the home aerodrome?

"Might as well," he reflected. "We've already overstayed our time." Pointing gently downwards, he suffered himself to drift. That is, if one in the midst of a blinding storm and seated in a war-plane may be supposed to drift. Rather it was being tossed about, constant vigilance at the controls alone keeping his plane from literally flopping over and somersaulting here and there, like a dead leaf.

Then without warning he felt the machine dropping down, down, down. Yet the planes were level and the whole natural resisting power of the machine was at its usual operation.

"By George! This storm has made an air cave underneath. I must get busy."

Another twist of the levers and the plane jumped forward, for the first time feeling no resistance of the storm. And, while he was glancing around for more light, out he shot like an arrow from a bow into the clear sunlight, the earth near—too near, in fact.

Back of him the storm clouds were whisking themselves away so rapidly that the transition was almost staggering. And below—what was it he now saw?

For answer, almost before his own mind had sensed the change, there came the spatter of Archies by the dozen and the menacing roar of machine guns, sheltered here and there over the scraggy plain within the pill-boxes that have of late been substituted for the vanishing trench lines. Artillery bombardments by the Allies have so devastated certain regions that trenches have become impossible; hence the concrete pillboxes.

"Lucky I've some gasoline left," thought Erwin, surprised but not unduly alarmed. "It's a race now between me and the bullets."

Instantly he put on high speed, at the same time rising in zigzags while the bombardment continued increasingly.

Right ahead, however, he saw what looked like a communicating underground trench; and at certain intervals were openings. These openings revealed to him a blurring, moving mass, muddy grey, yet with glints here and there as of some substance brighter. Closer yet he flew, regardless of safety. His air tabulator was not working. That was a sign that he was within two to three hundred feet of the earth. All at once something flashed out from this moving mass that presently disappeared underground again.

Archie had momentarily stopped. But an unmistakable whistle of lead was accompanied by a metallic puncture below. The bullet hit the near end of his petrol tank almost at his knee. Now he knew.

"Lordy!" he palpitated. "That's too near!" Already his fingers were twisting the speed accelerator, while up went the nose of his machine. Still the Archies spake not, but the spat, spat, spat of real rifle bullets followed his retreat.

Just then his hand, feeling below, came in contact with the hand grenades which he had forgotten amid the excitement of his later flight. Ahead rose a swell of land that he knew terminated in a bluff abutting upon one of the smaller streams of that region. This underground trench, evidently dug at great cost of labour and life, went straight for that bluff.

Their own aerodrome lay only a few miles opposite.

By actual and repeated reconnaissance both from below and in the air, this bluff was considered as deserted, or held at most by a very small force. This was owing to its supposed isolation.

Evidently Erwin had just made a great discovery. At least he hoped so.

On he flew. His machine was hit in many places, principally the wings, the tail and along the under side of the fuselage. Through this had come the ball that nearly perforated the tank.

There was one more opening ahead and then the trench sank out of sight near the base of the low bluff. Orry's hand closed over the first grenade. He was really an expert bomb-thrower. At great risk he dipped gradually until, when about at the point overhead he desired, he threw two bombs in swift succession. Then–up, up rapidly. With all the power of his engine he climbed, while two sharp explosions sounded from below.

Had the lad looked down he would have seen the trench walls at the open space crumble inward, while the mass of moving grey appeared to disintegrate, to vanish for the time being.

But with the throwing of the bombs, Erwin had other work on hand. Archie had broken loose again. One larger moulded shot ripped through the tail of the Bleriot, ricocheted obliquely and hit that same tank again, but with more force. His head lowered, the lad saw what had been done. More than that he saw what impended. The petrol was low.

Being under fire, at any moment a stray shot might ignite what little was left. Pointing the machine still more upward, he seized a bunch of loose lint, used to sop up recurring leaks here and there, and with a handy screw driver he managed to stop the rent in the metal with a few sharp adroit punchings.

Again to the machine, now over and beyond the bluffs; over the crinkling muddy stream, now almost overflowing its banks. On the bluff behind a squad of men in grey were training one of the Archies that had been dragged up from somewhere underneath.

"I've got to give her all the head she'll take," he thought. "That gun will get me if they understand their business."

Over beyond the stream a low embankment rose well up at perhaps three to four hundred yards from its first bank. Erwin was rising in a steep climb, zigzagging crazily for the machine was giving out, owing to lack of fuel. But he made a last effort to thus dodge the rain of bullets that began to pelt upon him from the rear. Another larger gun came up. Both joined in firing.

A shell splinter struck his shoulder, tearing loose the leather garment, while a searing, hot agony seized him, paralyzing his left arm.

He was over the second embankment when the final crisis came. Were these foes or friends that were popping up, pointing weapons at those behind? Friends surely! Down he had better go. The pain was so acute that only one arm was now at his service, while the dizziness that accompanies the pain of severe gun wounds filled his brain, dimmed his eyes, palsied his last despairing effort to land somehow behind that sheltering embankment.

Just then came a last explosion close behind. He seemed to be going down, down—where?

Then a terrific shock, and all consciousness left him. The shock seemed to drive from him all notion of anything or anybody. He knew nothing, nothing—nothing —

When at last Orris Erwin again knew that he was in the land of the living he was in a base hospital behind the front, and not far from his own aerodrome. His shoulder was in bandages. His left arm was in splints, but not painful. What seemed to be other bandages swathed his lower legs. Altogether he felt himself to be in pretty bad shape.

Then appeared Sergeant Anson who, seeing that Erwin was now awake and sensible, paused, a dry grin upon his weatherworn visage.

"Huh! Where's that Bleriot you or Blaine were to bring back?"

But the smile that accompanied this was not condemnatory by any means.

"I stuck to it, sir, long as I could stick to anything. How do I happen to be trussed up this way here?"

For a first reply the Sergeant threw back his head and gave vent to a real laugh. Then he patted Orry's curly head gently.

"You'll know in due time, youngster! Where's your pilot, Lafe Blaine?"

"Isn't Blaine back, too, and in that Death's Head Boche plane he—we took from them back of their lines? As for the Bleriot, I was in it last I remember."

Here the door of the ward opened, and who should walk in but Blaine himself, with Monsieur Cheval following. Cheval wore upon his breast a silver medal resembling nothing so much as an ace. For a wonder Blaine himself wore a tricolour ribbon with a tiny gold cross that Erwin was sure he had never seen his athletic countryman have before.

At sight of Erwin's pale face and rather fragile form, now animated with conversational fire and energy, the big American turned to his French comrade, saying:

"There, my friend! Did I not tell you that our brave little comrade would be more like himself today than he has been any time these ten days? Say little one," bending over Orry affectionately, "have you got over that nasty spell yet? Ha—I guess so!"

"Where's that Bleriot the Sergeant said we must bring back? I was in it when—when the Boches or—or the devil got me."

"That Bleriot, like yourself, mon comrade, is in the hospital; that is, the repair shop." This from Monsieur Cheval, still wearing his right arm in a sling, though now divested of splints.

"Oh!" A flash of dim recollection came to Orry for a moment, "I kind of remember. First there was a bluff, with what looked like a communicating trench, in spots. Just as if most of it was covered. I dropped some bombs I had left on the moving grey something I saw. After that I skimmed over the bluff. Then there was a stream, and another embankment beyond. After that I don't seem to remember much. How did I get here?"

"You got here, Orry, because the Boches downed you right over our front trench at this angle, which is nearer the Boche line than anywhere in this sector. We didn't even know that the enemy had dug a covered trench to the far side of the bluff on the river bank until you let us know by dropping bombs on them. This so angered them that they dragged out two Archies and peppered you good. You fell into our trench, and—and with the knowledge you gave us we directed our heavy artillery right on that bluff."

Here Blaine grinned complacently while patting Orry's head again, very gently though, on account of the bandages.

"Yes, *mon* comrade," supplemented Cheval. "It was to you that our batteries owe their accuracy of firing in dealing with that bluff. Do, you know that they must have been digging there for days, perhaps weeks? The whole interior had been hollowed out, and there was a picked battalion stationed there. La, la! It was a lucky accident that led you in my own good Bleriot to lay open to us the secrets of those over yonder, who are trying to enslave the world."

"But—but I didn't know," murmured Erwin gratified, yet somehow feeling as if honours were being heaped gratuitously on his undeserving head. Something of this escaped him the while. Monsieur Cheval held up a protesting hand.

"No, no! You must not! You shall know what France thinks of the service you have done for her, and—yes, for your own brothers-in-arms as well. Listen! You are already promoted, Monsieur Erwin. I may tell you that much. And so is your comrade, Blaine. Look! He already wears his decoration."

"Oh, well," said Orris wearily, "we didn't do so much after all. We did our bombing—what we were sent to do. Then we somehow had to go down in back of the Boche lines. While there we took that German machine. It was right handy, and no trouble. What else could I do but bring back your Bleriot, leaving Lafe here to do all the work of fetching in that Boche machine and the Boche himself? Got back all right, did you, Lafe. Looked to me when that other crowd tackled us as if you might have your hands full."

Blaine here smiled, nodded, and playfully rejoined:

"Looked to me as if you, too, would have some time getting back. And I guess you did too, by the way you look now."

All this was vaguely complimentary, yet rather overdoing the thing, or so Erwin seemed to feel, for he sighed and turned on his pillow as if weary.

At this juncture the ward door again opened and there walked in several uniformed men who had just stepped out of a military car, visible through the temporarily open door.

One of these strode forward, while the rest followed. This

foremost one was of distinguished appearance and bore on arm and shoulder the insignia of a French general. The others were also in uniform, except for one who wore a frock coat.

Just at this minute another door opened and there entered a tall, squarely built form in United States khaki, but without decoration except for the stars of a major general modestly affixed to his straight, stiff coat collar.

"Why, there's General Pershing!" whispered Blaine, keeping his hand at the salute which he had intuitively begun upon the appearance of the French.

"Petain and Pershing!" gasped Orris to himself, yet turning wearily from a futile attempt at saluting like the rest.

The two commanders greeted each other cordially, though the meeting was rather unexpected on the part of both. Each had heard of the night bombardment which had taken place only a few days back. Pershing was on his way to some American billet not far from here. Petain, having already received reports of the recent exploits of the two airmen, and having decorated Blaine, was now bent upon doing similar things for this wounded American lad who had unwittingly been of such service to the French along its sector.

In a kindly and unassuming way Petain, now reinforced by the presence of the American general, complimented Orris on what he had done, concluding with: "Not only did you and your comrade capture and bring home a German aviator and his machine, but you have sent two others in the earth and, after all this, while hard pressed by the enemy, you managed to descend upon the foe right where they were preparing for secret attack. This you frustrated, at great physical cost to yourself. For all this my Government bestows upon you this decoration."

While all the staff looked on, with nurses and flyers respectfully in the background, the general pinned on Erwin's breast a decoration similar to that bestowed upon Blaine. Continuing, the general said:

"When you are again able to rejoin the squadron, you,

like your friend, will find that your own government has not only approved, but rewarded you also for what you have done. Farewell!" The general with his escort left. General Pershing stopped only long enough to shake hands informally with those remaining, particularly with Cheval, Blaine and finally with Erwin. Walking with Sergeant Anson towards the door, the general turned, saying over his shoulder:

"It wouldn't surprise me a little bit if the heads of the American Corps at Washington did not send you two something in the near future. If they do, try and live up to it. Good-bye!"

He was gone. Monsieur Cheval had also followed, more slowly.

Blaine and Erwin looked at each other meaningfully.

"Reckon anything will happen, Lafe?"

"How should I know, Orry? Wait awhile and see."

Ten days later arrived two war medals, and two appointments; one for Blaine as sergeant in the aviation corps, the other for Orry as first corporal in the same.

CHAPTER 5

The Practice Drill

About the time that Corporal Orris Erwin was able to take his place again as a fighting aviator, Sergeant Blaine, returning from a long scouting raid over in the enemy's territory, met the boy in the broad drive of the aerodrome looking about him rather strangely. He threw an arm over Orry's shoulder, and drew him along to the door of the Aero Club.

"Been in here?" he asked. "It is great! They asking 'bout you the day we left. Heard about Cheval?"

Orris, not feeling like talking, shook his head, vouchsafing:

"Nothing only that he went along with your squadron at the last minute."

"Poor chap! He won't raid with us again. He went down near Essen. There was where we were to unload most of our bombs. But Archie got him. Down he went—" Blaine's eyes grew moist at the memory.

Erwin understood. "Nothing more?" he ventured.

"Nary thing, except that we gave the Krupp works hell for about fifteen or twenty minutes. You should have seen the explosions."

"That part was good. Say, Blaine," Orris, was looking, thoughtful, "has it ever struck you how terribly uncertain a thing life is —"

"Oh, rats!" Blaine shook his smaller companion as they neared the club door. "Stow that sort of talk and thought! Don't do you a bit of good or those that hear you. See?"

"Still, since my last flight with you, these thing will run across my mind. What is up now? You in on anything yet?"

"I've heard—but don't whisper a word—that we're on for a job of sausage driving next. Nothing sure, though."

Sausages is the slang term for gas observation balloons which go up at certain points and observe the enemy's positions or manoeuvres before and during battle on the earth below. Sausages do not fight back much but are protected by support battle planes and in other ways.

Reaching the clubroom door, they entered, Blaine pushing his comrade forward and saying with mock politeness:

"Let me present my comrade Erwin, or Orry, I like to call him. While doing the Boches the other day at Appincourte Bluff, the Boches came mighty nigh doing him. But here he is, what's left of him. Jolly him a bit. He feels bad!" The last tweak in allusion to Orry's remark on the uncertainty of life.

'There were a dozen or more of the air lads in the room and cigarette smoke tinged the air. Towards Erwin, now recovered after nearly a three week's "lay-off" on account of his burns and other wounds, there was a general rush of friendly hands and voices.

"Oh, you bully l'ill boy! If I hadn't been kept so busy would have gone round to jolly you up a bit. But I kept hearin' from you all the same."

This from Milton, or "Milt" Finzer, a Louisville lad, now in the Royal Flying Corps for more than a year. "Don't it seem wallopin' to see you in the clubroom again!"

"Orry, you stale mutt," this from an Americanized Pole, without a trace of foreign accent, "I'm too glad to see you to talk much about it. When we bombers got back from the raid that night and neither you nor Lafe had showed up, I felt bad enough. Later when Lafe came in with a German plane and a half dead Boche inside, we felt better. But we missed you, Orry."

"Did you really and truly miss me?" Erwin asked, this not in a spirit of doubt or incredulity, but only to hear his friend reemphasize it. One likes at times to have welcome truisms re-echoed over again. It is human nature I suppose.

"Look here, Lex Brodno, you're a Pole —"

"Don't spring that on me again, even in joke I am an American, it my folks did come over from Warsaw."

"Bully! We're all one over here. That's the way to talk!" Erwin was getting back his old-time spirits. "All one in the good old U.S. All one over here—eh? Oh, you sinner!" The two walked over to a table, interrupted at every turn by those who wanted to welcome Orry back to the club again.

The following morning Erwin resumed his daily stunt of practice, but was heightened mightily in spirit by noticing in the hangar where he had usually gotten his machines a bright new scouting plane, small, with a tail like a dolphin's, an up-to-date machine gun mounted along the top, just where the one pilot at the wheel could handily squint through the sights.

"Why, it's British—one of their latest makes," informed Erwin, much pleased. "It's—let's see." He was squinting at the monogram. "B-X-3. No. 48."

Just then Blaine and Finzer strolled up.

"Going out for a little spin, Orry?" queried Blaine, throwing open wider the hangar door. "Look at 'em! Ain't they beauts?"

There was a row of eight of these snug-built machines, all the same type and monogram, all with machine guns strapped solidly to the fuselage of each, and with motors of great power and pliability.

"You can do anything with these chaps," remarked Milt, "except fly to the moon. But these motors would take you a long way. As for stunts like diving, circling, dipping, playing dead and the like, you never saw the like. I only hope we go out soon. I learn there's a new raid on the taps."

Blaine was nosing about one of the machines that was like the others, only a trifle larger and had an observer's seat behind the pilot's.

"That's your, Sergeant?" queried Erwin, slightly emphasizing the last word.

"Bet your bottee wootees, Corporal!" Another slight emphasis on the last word. "As for yours, take your pick. They're all exactly alike. We must go into preliminary practice today."

For an answer Erwin mechanically rolled out the machine he had first examined, and prepared for a short flight.

"After all, all, these are much like the planes we used at Vimy last year."

"Some improvements and stronger motors added thought," said Blaine. "Going to give it a try-out?"

"Yep! Thought I'd like to get my hand in a bit before we go out in squad formation." He nimbly vaulted into his seat over the rim of the fuselage, or the body of the machine, as two mechanics pushed forward behind the wings.

An upward flip and the alert planes rose gently into the air, and Erwin was off. His head was cool, his brain active, and more than all his hands were steady.

About this time Finzer had rolled out another plane and almost immediately rose behind Orris.

The two were at once climbing high, higher, until at an elevation of two to three thousand feet they began to circle, climb and dip in a way that reminded one of two high-flying birds playing at tag far up in the blue expanse of sky above.

Then Erwin's machine did a flip, bringing it above the other machine and "onto its tail," the favourable position for aerial attack. Suddenly Finzer turned his nose earthward and began a whirling dive. Erwin followed; the other coming at once into horizontal poise, turned his nose towards Erwin—the perfect position for pouring a rain of shot as the other passed.

Of course all this was mere practice, the full handed exercise of the fighting aviator, through which he keeps brain, eye and hand in trim against the perilous, heroic few seconds when he must fight to save his life and machine.

Meantime Blaine, along with Brodno, the Americanized Pole, and one or two others, strolled about, lazily watching the manoeuvres above, and telling stories more or less related to their and fighting experiences flying.

Presently down came the two fliers, each with heightened colour and full of that fresh buoyancy which short, lively flights are apt to create. Both were flippantly arguing as to which one had got the best of the other.

"I own up that I am a little bit stale, Milt. But you wait until we go out for squadron practice. I'll show you!"

"Yes, you will," replied Finzer, good-naturedly caustic. "Perhaps I'll show you another trick or two then."

And so the chaffing went on as the lads adjourned to the eating-house for lunch.

This meal over, a bugle sounded from the parade ground near the grove of trees. It was the general summons for squadron practice. As the boys filed out, each in full flying rig, they saw Commander Byers on the field, watching the mechanics roll out the machines. There were a dozen or more of the fighting planes, like those which Erwin and Finzer had used for morning practice. In the east, from over a monotonous expanse of scarred and war-torn country, came the sullen roar of artillery at the front, a stern reminder that real war was close at hand.

Each aviator at once mounted his own machine, Blaine as squad sergeant in the one he had indicated to Erwin earlier in the day. Erwin took his, while Finzer, Brodno, and a real American lad from Butte, Montana, were assigned to others of these fast, nimble, scouting planes that are really the wasps of the air, carrying their sting with them, always ready and willing to bite.

Meanwhile at each machine two mechanics, under the eye of the airman, went carefully over the mechanism until all were satisfied. Up they went, singly or in pairs, gyrating playfully, always climbing, and swooping higher, higher, until to the naked eye they became mere dots in the clear sky.

By this time it was noticeable that they had somehow divided into two squads or escadrilles; and at a signal from Commander Byers down below they began manoeuvring like two hostile squadrons about to engage in aerial battle.

Thereupon ensued a display of battle tactics that would have been bewildering to an unaccustomed spectator.

These vicious little fighting planes reminded one more of air insects than of birds. In their forward rushes many of them were doing more than two miles a minute.

"Watch out!" said the Commander, his glass at his eyes. "The Sergeant is going to loop."

True enough, Blaine's machine took a nose flip. He was riding upside down. Then he was level again. The rest of his squad followed suit, then followed their leader at a daring angle, all of them straight and level again. The first plane in the other line, driven by Erwin, began to loop the loop side-wise, rolling over and over, not unlike a horse rolls over when turned out to grass. The others behind him began much the same tactics while the first line drew away as if preparing for counter moves.

Beyond, in the further sky, two opposing machines having detached themselves from the rest were playing with each other like kittens with wings. One was making rapid evolutions, the other following, and clinging to the set course in a series of whirls with its own wing-tip as a pivot.

Below, the comments went on from the staff surrounding the Commander, who would say now and then:

"Look you there! Was that not fine?"

"Hard to beat," seemed to be the general verdict. "Fritz will have to open his eyes tomorrow."

And so the show above went on. A flock of little birds chirped and flopped past the group below. What pikers they seemed by comparison, with the show going on above—far above! And now they were descending in long spirals, each squad by itself, yet preserving the mathematical distance re-quired, both from the opposing squad and at the same time keeping the line prescribed for such tactics during drills at the home grounds.

Particularly did Blaine distinguish himself in the daring of his stunts. Erwin was hardly behind him. They looped again, they rolled, they did the wing and tail slides, doing the last until they fell almost perpendicularly a thousand feet. Finally they righted hardly two hundred feet above the earth; then shot upward again at almost incredible speed.

And now the two leaders circled slowly as their respective squads followed on towards the ground, some falling, drifting like dead leaves, others slanting lazily as they passed the leaders, and on down, alighting at last each in his appointed place or thereabouts.

And then the two leaders began circling and swooping more and more rapidly until those below felt the whirring rush of air as the two planes swept by so low that one imagined that an arm would nearly touch them.

All hands knew it was rivalry—the rivalry of stunts. Yet to stand below and watch those steel engines falling down on you from the skies took the same kind of nerve to keep from dodging as only airmen themselves are gifted with by practice.

Finally all this drew to a close. The machines at last ranged themselves at opposite extremes of the landing stage and with a final swoop both were apparently upon the spectators as with the rush of a whirlwind. Yet, dizzy as it looked, it was mathematically timed. The two planes flattened as if by magic; they rose, dipped again and, passing each other in the down grade, saluted methodically as they passed the Commander. Ten seconds later their wheels dropped gently on the gravel at either end of the parade ground two tired looking aviators left their the waiting mechanics and walked soberly to the others.

The stunts were over for the day.

CHAPTER 6

Catching the Spy

"Well, well, Orry! How do you feel after your stunts of yesterday?"

This from Sergeant Blaine as he jumped from his bunk in the aerodrome dormitory the following morning just as the dawn was breaking.

Erwin, still drowsing, opened one eye. The next instant, remembering what the day probably hold in store for him, he threw off the covers and leapt from his bunk. At the same time, in order impress Blaine with his general fitness, he hit the big Sergeant a mock blow on the midwind region where, according to ring history, Fitzsimons dropped Corbett in their historic championship fight. Then he sprang back, arms and fists feinting.

"Can't you see how I feel?" he retorted. "Want to try me more?"

"Nit, you shyster, nit!" Blaine was laughing as he recovered, retreating and grimacing, as if in mock misery. "I don't want no more solar plexus stuff at this stage of the game. I guess you're all right."

"Bet your thick cocoanut I am! I was a bit drowsy at first. Say, Lafe, you know I must be in on this, whatever it is."

"Sure! I was at first a bit afraid that all those air stunts might have frazzled you a little, seeing you are just out of hospital."

"Honest Injun, Lafe, I'm all right! Don't you forget to re-member that!"

"Well, then, get your clothes on. I want to talk to you private like." And Blaine sauntered off, lighting, a cigarette, while Erwin hastily put on his clothes. Going out soon, he encountered Blaine on the parade before the hangars where the starting of planes usually began.

It promised to be a lovely day. Not a cloud was in the sky. Off to the east a lone airplane was, soaring high over No-Man Is-Land, doubtless one of the night scouts that are maintained along that portion of the front.

Said Lafe:

"Last night after the rest of you had gone to the clubroom, Byers sent for me and told me briefly what he wanted us to attempt today. You know those sausages the Boches got now, over back of that bluff you unearthed the day you came home after our last raid?"

"Appincourte?" Orris blinked and nodded. "I ought to remember."

"Well, the French have tried a time or two to get them, but the Boche planes have been too much for them so far. Kept them so busy fighting back, they had no time to do much bombing. And now word has come from headquarters that they must go. Must! See?"

Erwin nodded. He took a deep breath, feeling already the lift in the pure morning air. Blaine continued:

"Well, Anson was to have headed this raid, but he's been promoted also. He's an ensign now. I am in his place and they made you corporal under me for two reasons. One was on account of the stunts you did along with me; then for what you did after you went on your own hook and busted into that Boche communicating trench which made them try to Archie you and thus exposed to us what they had done in making themselves at home under Appincourte Bluff."

"Yes, yes! Come to the point, Lafe! What is it you and I have got to do today, or whenever it comes off?"

"Don't be so impatient. The second reason is because they now think you have nerve enough for most anything, and that we two, working together might succeed in puffing off this sausage business best in our own way."

"You mean we are to bomb them where and when we please?"

"No—of course not! But Byers, who is the real head here, thinks you and I, taking as many other chaps along as we please, can force our way in our fighting planes to where these pesky gas keep hanging and spying on us, and literally blow them to dashed smithereens. See?"

"But how? Their Archies will blow us to Hades and be gone before we reach anywhere near. It looks like a forlorn hope —"

Blaine smiled, as he interrupted with:

'Like Balaklava, eh? Or old Pickett's third day charge at Gettysburg?'

Erwin did not reply. Blaine continued:

"If we go strong enough and swift and low enough, we'll got there; and, once there we'll do the bombing all righty!"

"And in broad daylight, too?"

"I don't say that, Orry. All this is strictly between you and me. Byers rather favours a daylight raid as affording a better chance to regain our own lines, either after bombing or in case we fail. But we're not going to fail . These dratted sausages have got to come down!"

"Are you sure they stay up at night?"

"Ever since we busted up that bluff you exposed, there they stay day and night, half a dozen or more. And my own notion is that if we have a new offensive here, which I think looks likely to a man up a tree, those blamed sausages will give the Boches too much leeway in nosing out ahead what we might be trying to do in getting ready."

"Well, what else? Will Captain Byers leave it to you? "

"I think he will . Having tried every other way and failed, he will let us—you and me in private but me in public, decide upon the way we'd prefer. Both of us have been over the ground. We know how far we have to go. I also know

131

about what the Boches have got behind those balloons. It was only a few miles from there that we—you and me—got that Taube and the German aviator. Believe me, unless things have changed mightily, there isn't much there in the way of reinforcements or more planes or anything."

"You've been back there since?"

"You bet! Finzer and I went over there the day before you left the hospital. The Boches have no notion that our side is doing anything here, except air-raiding in No-Man's-Land or using our planes. That is one reason the headquarters thinks that it is a good place to—to do something."

"Well Lafe," Orris spoke deliberately, "you know I am with you. Tell me as much or as little as you please. I'll follow you to the last notch."

"I knew it!" Blaine grasped his comrade's hand and nearly wrung the fingers off. "Well, keep mum! Don't say anything to anybody but me. If Byers says anything, give him to understand you are in it from the word go, but no more. We'll win out again. Hear me?"

For reply, Erwin shook his released fingers, regarded Blaine with mock reproach, and volunteered:

"I'll agree to everything after that grip, I'm with you to the death. But don't do that again."

Blaine laughed gleefully as he turned away, patting Orris on the shoulder approvingly.

"I always thought you were a sticker, Orry."

"That's better 'n being a slicker or a slacker, isn't it?"

Again the big fellow laughed as he hurried off towards the Captain's quarters at the far end of the grounds.

The day passed quietly. From time to time, Blaine held private conferences with various members of the flying squad. These were mostly Americans who had either served a year or two at the western front, or were more recent arrival who had joined because of special aptitude for flying.

During the day sundry scouts penetrated here and there over the enemy lines and their report were favourable for the plan Blaine had in mind. A risky plan, yet promising well if skilfully carried out.

Towards night he had a last conference with Byers, who had more than hesitated over the proposed program, yet gave in before the Sergeant's enthusiasms.

"I agree," said the commander. "But it is risky. It can be done. Yet whether you are the man to do it—well, we'll know in the morning. Do your best. Be prudent; not too prudent; but at the same time try to be wise to things as they come up. Remember I have more responsibility than you. Your responsibility is only to me. It ceases where mine begins."

"Don't fear, Captain. Let what Erwin and I did the other night be duly considered. I need your full support —"

"Young man, you have it!" Here Byers took Blaine's hand and shook it heartily. "Bring back as many of your squad as you can, but above all carry out your program."

Night came, and with it a comfortable fog that rose white and misty, good for the purpose in hand. The clocks were pointing towards seven when something like a dozen men, wearing the regulation uniform, gathered at the usual open space, while from the doors of several hangars mechanics were silently rolling out machines.

Each aviator gave a few comprehensive looks and touches to his own plane, just to reassure himself that things were all right. Then came a brief moment or two of silent waiting. There were no, spectators. Even the rest of the men at the aerodrome did not appear. This was according to orders.

Out in front stood Captain Byers, attended by Blaine and Erwin, talking in low, indistinct tones. Finally Byers looked at his watch.

"Time's up, I guess. Do your best, you two. You, Blaine, will veer to the right as you approach the enemy trenches. You, sir," to Orris, "will draw to the left. Your squads will follow their respective leaders. Should you meet opposition before you reach the balloons, don't flinch. Pour on more speed. Don't signal unless necessary but obey signals when given. *Au revoir*, lads! Don't come back until you have delivered the goods."

Back went the Sergeant and Corporal, each to his own machine, which headed a short double line holding six planes, or a dozen in all.

At a quiet signal the leaders rose, spiralling into the upper darkness. Presently all had vanished, zigzagging in an easterly direction. About this time there came a sudden blue flare as a solitary rocket shot upward from beyond the grove of trees that that marked the landing place within the enclosed area that formed this aerodrome.

Instantly Byers was on the qui vive, he being nearest the point indicated by the blue flare. Bursting into a full run, he sped towards the spot, at the same time breaking in on several sentries unobtrusively posted about the grounds where the raiders had departed.

"Scatter lads!" he ordered. "Hurry! Spies at work! Halt any one you see, no matter who! Bring 'em in!"

Never halting in his race, he made directly for the spot whence the flare of the rocket had gone up. As he neared the trees, the sounds of a child's voice came to his ears, just inside the grove. It was remonstrating to some one.

"D—don't, papa! I—I want to get the pieces. My! Wasn't it pretty —"

Another voice, hoarse, gruff, stopped the childish words, but what it said was indistinguishable. Byers looked around. Two of his sentries were near, all of them running.

"Did you hear that child?" queried the captain. "Scatter! Don't let either child or the grow one escape. Be spry! Watch out!"

As Byers uttered the last exclamation, a running figure emerged from the shadow of the nearer trees and started full tilt towards the quarters where the cook's galley was. All three, running hard had slightly scattered, in order to intercept the fugitive should he try to dodge amid the various buildings.

Swift as were the pursuers, the fugitive was more speedy.

At one instant they saw him in a twinkling of light from one of the open doors. The next instant the form was gone. There came a faint echo of half-smothered infantile cries.

Byers dashed by the lighted door, then stumbled over a small form on the ground and there rose another wail, now of terror if not of pain.

Quickly the captain picked up the small figure in big arms and ran on, holding it gently, yet firmly, and saying:

"There, there, little one! I won't hurt you!"

"D—don't you hurt my pa," wailed the small figure in his arms. "He—was only making show for me —" More crying.

Where was the man? Only one clew had the captain. The fellow was round-shouldered, or seemed so in the glimpse Byers caught of them just before he dropped the child. Presently, one after another of the sentries came in, breathless yet unsuccessful. Somehow the fugitive had vanished, and look as they might, no further sign of him was seen.

"Skip around some more!" ordered the captain. "Try every door you pass. The fellow must be around somewhere. Call me if necessary. I'll be on hand."

While the baffled sentries did as directed Byers who was a father himself, placed the child on a convenient bench beside him, patting its head soothingly with one hand while he searched his pockets with the other. Then he produced the remnant of a package of chocolate drops, part of the contents of a box recently received from home.

"Like candy?" he asked, putting some of the candy in the child's lap. "Good candy—right, from my home across the sea."

This in such French as Byers could command, which was plenty for the purpose. At first the child, whom he now perceived was a girl, would not try it, but presently a sight of the sweet was more than it could stand.

Seizing the offered sweets, it began to eat greedily.

"My papa have no sweets like this," munching greedily. "Who you? Where my papa?"

"Know where your pa stays? I take you back to him."

135

For an answer the girl jumped down, still clutching the candy. She took Byers' hand, leading him back by another alley amid buildings here devoted to the culinary department of that cantonment. One of the sentries appeared. The child pushed on, leading Byers, who cautioned the sentry to say nothing, but to follow.

"What is your papa's name?" asked the captain.

"He name Bauer—Monsieur Bauer —" The child suddenly stopped.

"What is the matter, little one?" asked Byers, pulses thrilling under a vague suspicion. But here the sentry, forgetting the captain's caution, interposed with:

"I know him, Sir! Hermann Bauer, our assistant quartermaster—"

'Hush-h-h!" admonished Byers, frowning, shaking his head and pointing at the child, now staring at him wonderingly, then pouting as she queried:

"You no hurt my papa?"

The door of a nearby house suddenly flew open and a fleshy, round-shouldered man appeared. He saluted, then said:

"Good evening, Messieurs! I see you have my little girl with you."

"Monsieur Bauer!" The captain stood up, ignoring the other's salute. "I suppose you know that you are now under arrest?"

"It is what I feared. May I take my little girl inside?"

"Yes, provided the sentry and I go with you."

"You may as well: you'll go anyway. Please do not give me away."

With remarkable nerve, Bauer lifted the wondering child to his arms and led the way inside.

Five minutes later he emerged, the captain and the sentry on either side, and set out amid childish protests from within.

"She overtook me while I was on my way," he confessed. "It is fate, I guess."

Then the three started on the way to aerodrome head-quarters.

About this time came the sounds of heavy firing over No-Man's-Land.

"That is one result of your rocket, Bauer, Byers, grimly.

CHAPTER 7

Downing the Sausages

Once clear of the Allied front line of trenches, the double platoon of planes spread out on either hand, flying swiftly yet keeping near the earth. This was strange for so formidable a squadron of fighting, one-man planes that usually soar up to lofty heights, far from the direct range Fritzy's Archies.

But their instructions were clear, and each trained pilot knew just what he had to do. Swiftly and still more swiftly they flew. The night mists, growing yet more opaque, promised, favourably. Appincourte Bluff, just beyond the little river, could hardly be seen at all, but the roar of the motors overhead indicated that something might be on the wing. Without question few advance sentries still remained near the ruins that once had been a capacious subterranean chamber. From there the Germans had doubtless expected to emerge in assault, while their artillery made the essential barrage to stay any possible resistance while their infantry crossed the stream. But the Allied bombardment, made possible by Erwin's daring final flight across the Bluff towards his own quarters, had made Appincourte futile so far as that assault went. Still Fritz might be there. He was there—that is, a few of him. They were watching for a signal—the blue flare of a rocket that should tell Fritz of another air raid.

But the noise of motors close above confused his calculations. Why were the Entente airmen flying so low? Might they not be up to more devilment with regard to Appincourte? The blue flare had gone up.

But it happened that Fritz did not see it. Fearing now that many bombs might be dropped their defenceless heads, and with the whir of many motors in their ears, all the time growing louder, nearer, the small squad of night sentries, scudded as one man for the small dugout. This had been made immediately after the Bluff was wrecked by the bombardment. In there they cuddled, expecting the deafening explosion of many bombs over or on their heads, determined to fly back to their advanced trenches at the first let-up of the expected deluge.

But no bombs descended. The motor thunderings passed, then dwindled, but towards the east. What did that mean?

Their sergeant was telephoning hurriedly as to what was happening: "Airplane motors close overhead. No bombing yet. Watch out."

Thus it happened that Bauer's first (and last) signal was rendered void insofar as it went. The raiders escaped the German fire for the time being. Moreover, they were puzzled. Why should the Allied "*schwein*" fly so low, yet do no harm where once they had wrecked things only a few days before? What were they up to, anyhow?

This query was not answered at once. The telephones roused the Huns in the front trenches. Yet it puzzled them, too. Hitherto the bombing on both sides had been done mostly from far above. Such skimming the ground across No-Man's-Land might mean anything.

Presently the thrum of approaching planes became more and more audible along that portion of the front.

From his plane Blaine made private signal to the others to put on all speed. Erwin did likewise. Consequently it was not a minute before the raiders were upon the front trenches, going at the rate of two miles a minute. Each man in those planes sat with an open nest of hand grenades within easy reach. The handle of the gun crank was handy, its deadly muzzle pointed along the top of the fuselage of each mobile plane.

Then a pistol shot rang out, and at the signal grenades were dropped as the now far extended line passed over those open trenches in which troops were massed. For, be it known, that fatal blue flare from the aerodrome a dozen or more miles away had filled those trenches yet more full of human cannon fodder. Hence the bombing was all the more deadly.

Passing the trenches, at another signal, the hostile planes nimbly wheeled, shot back again and poured forth more bombs upon those trenches. Still again they wheeled and traversed them for the third time.

By this time machine guns began to spatter their deadly contents among the darting planes, while further back the anti-aircraft guns gave forth searching roars as to what they might should a plane be hit.

It was enough so far as it went. Now for the gas-bags, the sausages; for these observation balloons were the real object of all this nocturnal pother.

"Forward!" came the signal again and, steering to the left, rising higher from the forty to fifty foot level they had hitherto kept, the squadron made for the rear line. Here rose a shadowy line of oval bags, so shaped as to qualify them for the term "sausage" as humorously fitted to these defenceless spying observatories. In daytime their elevation enabled them to see over a great expanse of that level, war-ruined region.

There they were, open carriages below, in each a small group of Fritzies with machine gun and bombs handy for use in times like the present. But here, too, Fritz was at a decided disadvantage.

Evidently no raid was anticipated, for here they swung, hardly half manned except by the few constituting the night watch. In and out among them shot the fast planes, the machines belching their deadly hail, with Fritz apparently too dazed by surprise to make much resistance.

Using explosive bullets that would flare sparks of fire at the moment of contact, soon those bags of gas were ignited, one after another. Down rope ladders the occupants climbed or dangled, dropping off to hit the ground maimed or lifeless. By this time, however, the Archies were pouring a rain of shells from the machine guns at the assailants with murderous and often fatal effect.

One plane after another sagged, lamely drooped and went to earth crippled or in flames. It so happened that Blaine and Erwin nearly met in, mid-air as each verged close in a final assault on the last balloon.

Seizing his megaphone, Blaine shouted:

"We'll down this one, then home!"

Bang—puff! A burst of flame enveloped the last sausage, and Blaine was already mounting higher, higher, when he saw Erwin's plane go zigzagging earthward at a gentle angle. One of his wings had been shattered, the remnants flopping as they fell. Orris, working at the controls, partially righted, then staggered on, and finally mounted upward, showing his chief that he would make the home trip if nothing further happened.

Blaine himself tried to follow. But something was wrong. He fell, half gliding, and finally landed with his planes too much shot to up for the machine to float longer.

"I'm a goner, unless something happens," he thought.

"Where was he? In that last staggering rise the sergeant was vaguely aware that just beyond some trees under him was an open space of some kind. Could he make that open space? The front enemy trenches and the line where the vanished gas bags had swung were behind him.

"Seems to me I saw one of our planes drifting over this way."

On earth it was darker, more misty, more impenetrable than it had been overhead. His watch, having an illuminated dial, indicated that the time was about ten o'clock. In his rear the darkness was more dense than ahead. Probably his plane had dropped just in the edge of that open space he thought he had dimly seen while up in the air.

While looking over his machine as best he could to see if

there was any chance to tinker it up so as to make another flight, he stopped short, his pulse leaping. Then he stood motionless.

"What was that?" he kept thinking, keeping as quiet as possible.

After a lengthy interval he heard rustling amid the trees near by, then a subdued crashing limbs, then an unintelligible moan or groan. After that came a heavy shock as if something or some one had struck the earth.

"I must look into this," he reflected, listening now also for any other sounds of human presence. But all was still near by. Back west there came the dying echoes of the recent scrimmage with the raiders. Hans, having gotten the worst end that deal, seemed to have subsided.

"Fritzy is preparing to look into things. He must know that some of us were knocked out. Doubtless he is getting ready for a more thorough look around."

Without formulating any definite plan, Blaine headed towards where the last sounds of some thing or some one falling had come from. To the left came the far rumble of trains crawling forward on one of the many side lines used by the Huns for war transportation.

From the right came the distant roar of heavy artillery, such as enlivens the front night and day. Yet it was so distant as to insure no connection with the finished air raid that now threatened disaster to himself.

Under the trees the darkness deepened, if such was possible. Where was he going? Could he find his way back to his own crippled plane?

A heavy, yet trembling sigh, terminating in a muffled groan, showed him his next course. Stumbling forward, he almost fell over a body prone across his path. Another groan, then:

"Oh-h-h, Gawd—Gawd!" Blaine thought he recognized something half familiar in the words or voice.

Stooping down, he felt a horrible slime and a mashed something that was not like anything he had ever felt before.

He dropped to his knees, drew out his small flashlight, hitherto held in reserve for desperate emergencies, and cautiously turned it on.

It glimmered across a face—a face at once familiar and horrible. A well-known face, yet so ghastly in its bloody disfigurement that Blaine shivered, drew back, then bent downward and forward.

"Finzer!" he gasped. "My God! Is this you?"

The one eye left faintly opened and the gashed lips muttered, though Blaine shuddered as he saw by the flashlight that the man's face and head were so torn by machine gun spatter that it was only a question of minutes, if not seconds, before he would be dead.

As it was, Finzer's one eye recognized his sergeant. He tried to speak, but vainly. Finally, with an effort that must have been a last clutch at his vanishing strength, he flung his mashed and bloody hand on a paper pad, with pencil laying by. One sentient gleam; then he gave up the ghost. What did Finzer mean by that last gesture?

With reluctance Blaine picked up the pad and read the following words now almost illegible with blood.

"Boche got me. Machine back by log pile. Good shape. Landed in tree. Done for. Saw you drift this way. Get machine if yours won't —"

Sadly Lafe drew the body of his friend aside, covered it with his leather blanket coat, piled brush over it, and drew meditatively back, saying:

"Poor Milt! It's all I can do for him now."

Again he scanned the pencilled lines, remembering that his own machine was in bad shape. "Maybe Milt's will do better. I'll see. Where's that log pile?"

His question was suddenly answered by his stumbling against something for he had already started on the search, having repocketed the tell-tale flashlight. No knowing when a stray ray might be seen by some enemy eye and its cause investigated.

Groping about, he discovered Finzer's machine half slanting down one side of the log pile. It had fallen through a tree top, hitting the logs. Milt, already blind, wounded unto death, had tumbled out, crawling a few feet, where he lay dying until Blaine heard and found him.

Swiftly Lafe righted and trundled the machine to a small, clear place. Risking the flashlight again, he briefly inspected it. Aside from sundry bullet perforations and certain unimportant scars in the wings, it was all right. The tank was pretty full yet, the interior mechanism in fair order, and the wheels propelling it in such good shape that Blaine soon had it back in the open space where he had been compelled to come down. As for the near-by woods, there was not much real life there. Long ago the ruthless shelling had reduced most of the timber to scraggy, scarred skeletons. Still they were dangerous to planes when trying to land—or to rise again. So he quickly transferred such of his belongings as he cared to save, placing them in Finzer's machine, and then assured himself that everything would work right when it came to rising again. All was ready. Another thought came.

"I ought to fire this plane of mine. Too good yet to fall into Fritzy's hands. He'd soon have it ready again."

Pushing Finzer's plane still further out m the open, he looked, listened, but still detecting no sign of human nearness, he opened the petrol tank of his plane, touched with a match the running liquid, and jumped nimbly to his seat in Finzer's machine. Applying the power, the plane rolled, skidded slightly then came to a full stop.

"What the mischief is the matter now?"

Out he jumped, vaguely fearful, while the other plane flared up brightly, the red flame mounting high, higher, scarcely forty yards away. In and out among the mechanism he fumbled, turned, twisted, adjusted, until from a distance came the sound of hoofs—galloping hoofs.

"Good Heavens! The Boches! They're coming? What will I do?"

As he asked this question his eyes, wildly distorted, roamed round the open space now lighted up for a hundred yards or more by the burning airplane.

Just then he happened to look upward, and all at once saw the cause of his present trouble. One of the longer limbs of an old, battle-scarred poplar, partly broken and hanging lower than usual, had caught in one of the top wings, thus halting him as he was about to rise.

"What a fool I am!" This while wrenching loose the ragged wing-end. "Let me get out of this somehow!"

Already he was again in his seat, turning on the power, swiftly yet surely manipulating the controls. The high-powered scout and battle plane rose with a rush and almost immediately began to climb, spiralling in long acute sweeps and turns.

"There they come!" breathed Lafe, venturing a last look around down below.

A field battery of horse artillery was emerging from the torn timber into the open space, which the burning plane had already showed Blaine to be a beet or turnip field of considerable extent. The constant roaring of artillery and a continuous red glow on the western horizon made known the cause of the uproar that had been growing for some time back.

"They're fighting hard," conjectured Blaine. "Guess wrecking them sausages must 'a' stirred Fritzy up a bit. Hullo! What's that?"

Already Lafe was a thousand or more feet up. The field battery was now fading from view as the flames of the burning plane died down.

CHAPTER 8

Blaine's Further Adventures

Once more sharp reports from the Archies came from below. Whether these were by the battery he had seen Lafe could not now tell. So thick was the fog, the gun flashings did not reach up to where he was now spiralling still upward, in order to get beyond the chance effect of some stray shot.

All along the now distant battle line the dull red glow of bursting shells lined the front as the rumble of sound jarred more clearly upon his ears. Undoubtedly some kind of battle must be going on. Was it one result of the night raid? Was Fritz, now that his observation points were at least temporarily out of active service, taking his revenge by another drive? And where the Allies would least suspect? That is, right over the Appincourte Bluff?

"What ought I do?" reflected Blaine, still gently climbing higher. "It's a still night, foggy, good for most anything up here, except to see or be seen and that's what I don't want. Wonder if poor Finzer had his night signals along? Ah, here they are!"

He was overhauling with one hand a small locker that was part of the fuselage Moreover, there were still two unused sheafs of ammunition for the Lewis gun and a few grenades and bombs. Finzer had not expended all his allotment in the balloon attack.

"Guess I'd better edge in towards where that drive seems

to be centring. That is the reason, probably, that this battery broke in where I was on the point of going up again. Fritz is up to some new thing, I'll bet."

Taking his bearings as best he could, Blaine headed more westward, keeping at an elevation of six or seven thousand feet.

"Wonder what they'll think back at the station when they don't find me among the ones that get back? Poor Milt! I lost my machine; he lost his life. And there were others, too. That Montana chap Bangs. Last I saw of him he was right under one of them sausages, letting Fritz have it with the Lewis. Looked like something would get him—heigho! What is that?"

Down below, slightly to his rear, there flashed through the fog a short series of varicoloured lights, which to Blaine's active mind spelled forth:

"Boches 'bout to get me. Big drive on hand. Yonder they go—watch out!"

That was all, but it was enough. Blaine knew that it must come from another of the raiding scouts who had somehow gone down in No-Man's-Land. It might come from a shell hole. Anyway, it was being sent up by some one risking almost certain death in order to let the Allies know that big things were already under way.

"Where are the Boche planes?" Blaine had more than once asked himself. The balloons were gone. The few enemy planes left to guard the gasbags had been put to flight by the daring raiders. Blaine himself had sent one down in flames. Others had followed the retreating raiders. Now that a night drive was on, other planes would be converging towards the salient thus suddenly selected for a night assault. In another instant Blaine's mind was made up.

"Here's at you, my friend," he said to himself. "I'll try to find out who and what you are. Damn the risk!"

With the thought he turned the nose of the triplane downward, so that it was almost at a perpendicular angle. Before this he had noted that around the point whence had risen that telltale signal there seemed to be a foggy void. This meant to Lafe that, for the present at least, there was nothing doing at this particular spot. Of course those signal lights might draw dangerous attention, but Blaine had resolved to risk the chances of that. Perhaps one of his comrades in distress had deliberately courted death or imprisonment m order to let their side know what was taking place. "Bully boy, whoever he is!" he thought.

Briskly yet carefully working his machine, Lafe descended until, when he flatted out, he could see through the fog the darker background of war-torn earth.

"I'll flash our private signal," he resolved. "He may see it. So may Fritz. But—here goes!" Lafe pressed with his foot upon a certain button that was connected with an electric flashlight fastened in a special groove at a downward angle of the fuselage or body of the car. At each pressure certain flashes emitted the message of inquiry in private code.

"Where are you, pal? I'm coming. Let me know if you can."

Circling round at an even slightly lower level, he continued to signal but without avail. Just as he was about to quit and rise higher again, he detected a faint red and blue gleam that apparently ceased without rime or reason. One faint glimmer succeeded, but died out as if suddenly broken off.

Without waiting for more Blaine gave a searching look around but, seeing nothing through the mist, gently, cautiously felt his way downward, easing up in speed as best he could. The wheels jolted over rough but level ground, until the nose of the plane shoved itself against an abrupt angle of rough earth that brought him to a halt all at once. Quickly he adjusted the controls and, revolver in hand, boldly leaped out.

Dark it was, except for the lurid flashings of distant artillery, while to the west the roar of infantry battle sounded much nearer than when Lafe was high up in the air.

"Where am I?" he asked himself, reaching for his pocket flashlight. "Surely this must be No-Man's-Land!"

Thus thinking, he stumbled against another plane; not his,

but the wreck of another one. Intuitively he felt that he must have landed right. Feeling round him, he detected certain signs that made him almost sure one of the raiding scout machines had fallen here.

"This must be one of those big shell holes," he thought. "Why—what if it is where those signals came from?"

Just as Blaine was about to climb up the incline of disrupted earth, his flashlight sending gleams here and there, a voice he recognized, sounded:

"Halt, you! I heard your motor, but you won't get me without a fight."

"Damn if it ain't Buck all righty," said Blaine, still climbing.

He turned his light to where the voice sounded, and bellowed, regardless of consequences:

"Don't you know your squad leader?"

"Good gracious! You—here?" The youth from Butte, Montana, was peering down at advancing form, delighted amazement in face, but he only said: "Shut off your light Sergeant! We're surrounded by—by—them! That's better! Where'd you come from?"

"Oh, I just dropped down in answer to your signal. I thought if the Boches were about to get you, they might have another chance at me, see?"

A faint yet hilarious chuckle came forth. Then:

"Say, Lafe, when I first tumbled down here, I thought I was a goner. But I wasn't hurt much. My machine is smashed, though."

"What brought you down? Why didn't you go a little further?"

"I would have, but Archie got me just as I thought I was about safe. That ain't all. I guess our downing them sausages was a bit too for Hans. Directly after that they started the hottest barrage fire you've seen in a month of Sundays. Keepin' it up yet, only they've slacked a bit along here. I kept thinkin' how I was going to get out of this when I heard the tramp and scuffle of advancing infantry.

"All at once I knew. They're sour yet over busting up their big underground at Appincourte Bluff; and now comes this raid of ours and away goes that string of a dozen balloons. I guess it was too much."

"Infantry! What infantry? Oh, you mean Fritzy!"

"Who else? Well, Fritz came with such a rush he didn't look for me. There was a lot of him passed. I scrunched down inside this crater the best I knew how and directly I knew I must let our folks know. Then's when I sent up my signals—in code, of course."

"That's so, Buck. I saw 'em and read 'em."

Buck was grinning to himself.

"You?" Bangs looked his astonishment. "Well, if we warned our folks in time, and I guess I did by the sounds, and then caught hold of you, it was a lucky venture."

"You caught me all right. But how are we going to get away? Say your machine is busted?"

"How'd ye know?"

"Well, by the way it came down and struck. I have no tools with me, and I had to crawl in here in a hurry."

"Come on," ordered the Sergeant in his official tone. "We've got no time to lose. I've got tools or rather Milt had."

"What's the matter with Finzer?" Buck was keenly concerned for he and Milt had been quite chummy.

Blaine told him briefly all that had happened.

"And you had to leave him back there? Well—well, it's war. Sure he was dead? By thunder! I'll get even yet with Hans—Gawd willin'. The skunks!"

All this and more while Lafe, now alert and busy, was getting out Finzer's tools. Presently the two were examining Buck's plane which they found was practically all right except for a big rent in two of the wings. With the appliances at land this did not take long, for both worked frantically, knowing that hostile planes from the neighbouring front would soon be hovering near and also that the infantry was due either to reform the battle line or, if not, that reinforcements might pass at any time.

In a very short while the job was done. To Blaine's surprise Buck began nimbly climbing back up the crater wall.

"Where ye going?" he gently called, but only heard in reply: "In a minute—in a minute!"

But while Blaine was fuming, still getting things in readiness, Bangs slid back down the embankment, dragging a shabby grey army overcoat. Lafe looked disgusted. He snatched it, held it up, flashed his light over it, then cast it down, saying:

"That's a Boche infantry coat—officer's, I reckon. What do we want of that? Get into your place. I've turned your machine round." Both climbed in, Bangs stowing in his own machine the coat he had delayed both to secure, a said the while:

"When those charging battalions went by, of their officers threw away his coat. They were on a double quick, to reinforce others that gone on before I came down.

"Lucky they happened to have no planes. Otherwise I'd never pulled through. As it was she was a close squeeze. I slipped down, bagged the coat, and here she is. You needn't laugh, Sergeant. There's maps and papers inside. Might be wuth something to our side yet."

"Bully for you, Bangs! I was wrong. Are you ready? Then follow me! We're going to stick round the Boche flanks a bit and who knows what we may run up against?"

Without a bit of trouble Blaine's triplane glided upward after a short slide over the rough level of No-Man's-Land, and he was off. Buck attempted to follow but the machine skidded sideways, struck a slope and after a mute struggle with adverse conditions came to a standstill. Cursing to himself, Buck jumped out, forced his plane to a more stable level, then mounting to his seat again he put on all power to try to overtake his companion. But in that short interval Blaine had vanished in fog.

"If this isn't bad luck, I don't know what is!" soliloquized Buck, as his Nieuport began to rise. "If I'd got off at first, I wouldn't 'a' lost Lafe. Well, I must do a trifle of scouting on my own hook."

Buck was climbing, not too fast, for he watched, still hoping that something might happen that he would sight Blaine again. Flying thus easily, climbing still higher, he was all at once startled by a burst of machine gun fire from the ground ahead. There came a reply higher up, and he felt that this must come from Lafe.

Mounting swiftly, he presently became conscious that a machine was hovering above and behind, "getting on his tail" as the slang runs among aviators at the front. The quickest way to avert the danger was first to try the "side loop" which is a kind of "loop-the-loop" sideways, a risky trick, yet a good thing if rightly done. Buck tried it instantly. When upside down he darted ahead swiftly but in a reversed course, bringing him fairly behind the other plane as he, righted.

As he came up to a level again, now behind his opponent, he saw for an instant that the shadow looming scarce fifty yards ahead looked strangely like Blaine's machine. What to do next—before firing? Use his private signal, of course. No sooner thought than done. Two peculiar flares shot forth, each glowing brightly for an instant, then vanishing.

"But—hey?" Bangs was ejaculating to himself excitedly. "Will he answer?"

Up, up climbed Buck, his pulses throbbing for one long instant, the nose of his machine settling rapidly on the tail of the other plane. Then came an answering flash. After that another.

"Bully for you, Lafe! My, that was a close call! I mustn't lose track of him again. We'll be there with the goods yet, if we stick together." This to himself.

Presently both machines were moving side by side, hardly fifty yards apart. To come closer at this rate of speed these small scouting planes maintaining would have caused a mutual air suction that might cause a collision. This is the real cause of many of the accidents that befall inexperienced aviators, when out flying, perhaps by themselves.

The night, of course, was far spent. The fog was lightening imperceptibly. Their watches betokened that it was nearing three a.m. Blaine got out his megaphone, for talking at high altitudes is much a matter of expanded lung power. He began, as usual, with a joke.

"Like to 'a' got you back there!" he shouted. "Where you been?"

"Looking for you mainly. What you going do next?"

"See that line of fire off norwest! We that's where our front and Johnny Bull's join. Appincourte Bluff seems either to have been turned or to have turned Fritzy off. Ready for a scrimmage?"

"You ought to know, Lafe!" Bangs laughed easily into the megaphone. "Ready for most anything."

"Well, our front there is rather weak. Follow me. Don't lose me. We'll give that infantry a time trying to find out who we are that's spitting on them from overhead. Catch me?"

"Yep-fire away! Suits me!"

In another few seconds the two machines were flying through the thinning fog, gradually lowering their altitude and nearing at a rate of a mile and a half a minute the advancing lines of the enemy, revealed only to these fliers by the close barrage fire maintained by their artillery in the rear.

Of course beyond this barrage must be certain observation planes. The chance must be taken of meeting one of these. Meanwhile the first thing was to begin upon the assaulting battalions with their machine guns.

Almost in an instant they were over the front platoons, flying as close as they dared in order to escape the barrage that was passing overhead, falling now behind the front trench line of the Allies. This in order to stop, or at least hinder the arrival of such reinforcements as could be thrown forward to strengthen this suddenly assailed point.

These planes, being of a late design, had a device whereby the aim of the Lewis gun could be instantly altered from a horizontal to a perpendicular slant. Moreover both Blaine and Bangs had repeating rifles, and revolvers. Great dexterity was shown by each as their machines, slackening their speed to that most suitable for accurate firing, their motors roaring right over the assaulting columns, poured down a spray of bullets that inevitably found a human mark.

Fritzy usually charges in dense masses. He is "cannon fodder"; he knows it, but apparently doesn't care. Now, however, he dodged, dived, hunted shell holes, and otherwise evinced extreme terror. First one plane, then the other, at nearest safe distance apart, rained down showers of death. Was this another repetition that earlier trench assault that resulted in the destruction of the sausages? It looked so. might also be other swift moving machines behind, each pouring leaden showers on infantry now defenceless. Yet a moment before they were placidly plodding on towards the death in front, for which they had been driven forth by their officers that night.

Occasional shots were fired upward by soldiers here and there. But though close, so swift were the machines that they vanished almost at once from the time of their first appearance at any given point.

Only two? No more. Fritzy began to take courage. Both planes were now whirring on somewhere else. But were they truly gone?

Even while officers were taking heart and again driving forward their men, back came the two planes upon their former path, but now going south instead of north.

Again were the former scenes repeated, with even worse results.

But now arose another sound, a sound as of an advance from the Allied trenches. What could be?

CHAPTER 9

The Final Fight

The two aviators, their planes much shot with holes but otherwise unhurt, rose suddenly, swooping in long circles to higher and yet higher altitudes. The first flushes of dawn were breaking. In the air two observation planes flying over the Allied front were signalling to the German batteries in the rear, from which came the barrage protecting their infantry from Allied advances. At once they knew what to do.

Both drove on through the hostile fire and bore down upon these observation biplanes. Observation planes are not good fighters. In less than a minute after rising those two fighting planes had chased the larger, slower machines off the ground.

But what was Blaine's surprise to see Bangs, not a hundred yards away, making bold signals strange code to the Germans back in the rear. Lafe himself could not read them. What did it mean? For an instant there flashed to him a suspicion that Bangs from Montana might not be just plain American.

"I won't think such a thing!" thought Lafe. "What is he up to?"

Then he saw that the enemy barrage was falling further back, just about where the recovering infantry was resuming its advance, after the short shock occasioned by the two raiding triplanes that had suddenly gone aloft.

"Were the Allies in their turn assaulting the Boches? What could it mean? In another brief interval Blaine found out,

155

when sudden demoralization set in at once. Without apparent cause the Boches, now nearly upon the first Allied trenches, found that they were the centre of a bombardment from the rear. What did that mean? The fire was withering.

Could the foe they were attacking be taking them in the flank? The idea was almost unbelievable. And yet the fire was also insupportable.

With one accord the front lines recoiled, although their officers beat the privates with their sword flats, cursing and reviling them as cowards. Right on top of this, the queer noises in front materialized into certainties.

The Allies were advancing. Were there not also reinforcements behind? Reinforcements hitherto kept back by what? The barrage. Where was that barrage now? Falling not only on their rear but also further back. How did this happen? Where were their own planes?

Officers and men were dropping on every hand. A charging foe in front was almost on them. After a minute or two of this, that whole section of the advance appeared to melt like froth on the water.

Meantime up above, and from a higher altitude than before, Bangs continued his mysterious signalling; not to Blaine or to the Allies, but—wonder of all wonders—to the Boches themselves.

Blaine now understood this, for he had noticed that the barrage itself had fallen back. Instead of covering and protecting the Germans, it was slaughtering them even more than the two aviators had done with their machine guns from a lower altitude.

Upon the sudden rout below, which was sensed rather than seen by the two fliers as the dawn rapidly grew, came the new rush of the Allies.

By this time Blaine felt that he and Buck must do one of two things. Those retreating observation planes would undoubtedly bring up air reinforcements. The barrage had already stopped. This was good for the charging Allies as well as the retreating Boches.

"Buck and I have either got to get back inside our lines or fight," he thought, carefully balancing his triplane against a rising breeze. "Or we might rise higher and take another chance. One thing we have done. We've helped bust up that charge, no matter how their advance has fared at Appincourte or elsewhere."

Forward went the Allied infantry, driving the now disrupted Huns before them. The fog kept clearing. Presently both Blaine and Bangs saw heavy masses of men advancing in platoon formation over the scraggy battle-scarred plain. They were probably two miles distant from the retreating Huns.

Blaine darted back and sent out his signal flares, announcing the fact. Indicating the probable distance, he waited for the barrage he was sure would come. Bangs, seeing that Lafe was signalling, doused his now useless Boche flares and confirmed what Blaine had signalled. Presently the barrage began, and now both saw that it was incumbent on them to remain up there as long as possible to assist the new Allied assault by rendering their barrage effective.

But Bangs once more perplexed Lafe by another manifestation of his way of fooling the Germans. More and more Blaine was perplexed.

"Where in sin did Buck get read up in Boche code flares like he is now? I know a thing or two, but he's got me beat to the woodpile this time!"

Bangs, spiralling upward and back towards the Hun front, was sending forth flare after flare that was meaningless to Lafe, yet which was for some purpose. Then suddenly Buck shot off on the side towards Blaine the following words in the code familiar to all Allied spad-pilots.

"Get back! Tell our folks to double their fire, keeping ahead of our advance. Savvy?"

Blaine mutely obeyed. The Allied fire was redoubled as per instructions. Buck, by this time far to the east, could now be seen making back towards the Allied front where Blaine was zigzagging to and fro waiting for what might come. Suddenly, behind Bangs, he saw the speck-like dots of Teuton planes emerging into the upper air and rapidly approaching. At the same time other planes in the west appeared, biplanes, scouts, and one or more heavy battle planes. Evidently the cards were being laid for a squadron air battle unless something else intervened. Instinctively Lafe thought of his ammunition roll. He was well supplied at starting on this trip, and had transferred his own remaining stock to Finzer's plane when abandoning his own. But the most of it had already been used. It was not likely that Buck was any better prepared in that line. At least they might wait and join their own planes, now coming out of the west.

In the east the hostile squadron came on rapidly. Deploying as they advanced, both Blaine and Bangs could see that there were battle planes, scouts, and heavy bombing machines. These last were sweeping lower, trying to get in range of the advancing Allies.

"Come on! Hurry up!" both aviators kept repeating to their own advancing air fleet. "No time to waste! Let's get at 'em. They're going to bomb our front lines."

Almost immediately a number of fast triplanes forged on ahead of the rest at a speed which a year before would have been deemed impossible. Joining the two weary airmen who had been up all night, yet were still full of the battle hunger, they swept low down and straight at the bombing planes, now beginning to drop their deadly explosives along the lines of advancing infantry. But only for an instant, as it were, did they go uninterrupted.

A hail of bullets from machine guns rained down upon them. In almost no time two of these planes went staggering earthward. Blaine, forgetting his almost empty sheaves of Lewis gun ammunition, hung upon the tail of one, while Buck, with side loops and a nose dive, flung himself almost literally on another.

"Holy Moses!" ejaculated Buck as his last full sheaf went

into the cartridge roll, and he realized that with this gone he would be absolutely helpless. "I don't want to quit. But if this don't fetch another one, I'll have to. I'll have to anyhow."

In the meantime, the Boche fighting planes had mixed in with the Allied fighters, interrupting their assault upon the bombers. And such an exhibition of diving, darting, nose dipping, looping, and what not had seldom been seen along that extended front.

Realizing the damage to be done by bombs on the unprotected infantry charging below, both Blaine and his comrade kept strictly after the bombing planes. Let those fresh arrivals who had plenty of ammunition attend to the fighting Fokkers and other battling planes that had arrived so inopportunely.

By this time the anti-aircraft guns were getting in their work. With the targets so close, though darting hither and yonder with bewildering speed, two of the German fighting planes were soon zigzagging towards the ground. One fell right in the path of a disorderly advance of the infantry, which happened to be a well-known Canadian battalion. From his perch, his own ammunition exhausted, Blaine saw those troops surge around and over that unlucky plane, then pass on, leaving a flaming wreck behind.

The bombs began to explode. Blaine saw the danger to other troops behind. It so happened that these troops were Sammies and Blaine, with a swoosh, swept down to within a dozen yards right over the heads of these men and the column heard his megaphone bellowing:

"Watch out, bunkies! 'Ware that wrecked plane! She's full of Boche bombs. Watch out—spread out! Give it room! Oh, you doughboys! Rah for Uncle Sam!"

Recognizing the meaning and divining that it must be an American, the Sammies shouted back as they divided and gave the necessary room:

"Oh, you Spaddy! What you doin' down so low? Rah for you! Bully boy! Rah, rah, rah! You're all right!"

159

And on they went, comforted themselves, and comforting the weary, ammunitionless aviator who now recognized that his present job was about over.

His plane was literally shot to pieces. The wings hung in tatters. Only the vital mechanism that kept him moving, thereby supporting him in the air, fortunately remained untouched. Even now he staggered and with difficulty rose a trifle upward, while off to the right he saw Bangs in even a worse fix.

The latter, with his wings honeycombed by bullet holes, had received the full charge of a machine gun from some passing battle plane in an around his propellers. His supply of ammunition too was now exhausted.

Could he make the ground in a safe place? With every ounce of power, his propeller crank revolving like lightning, still he made alarmingly slow progress. Good reason why. Two of his propeller blades were shot off. The other two were revolving swifter than can be imagined. He felt that he was drifting down, down, amid the riff-raff, smoke and confusion of a battlefield over, which the thunders of conflict had twice passed.

Above, the aerial battle was still going on, though making towards the east; for the Germans, following their retiring columns, were being slowly yet persistently pushed back to their trenches. Occasional bullets spattered about him. Day was fully on, and a rising sun disclosed a prospect of clearing skies.

There was a ruined house or cabin just ahead. Could he land there? It lay deserted for the time being amid war wreck and ruin, its roof battered in, its stone walls crumbling. Still it promised temporary shelter. Blaine had vanished. Had his plane gone down? Was he smitten by a stray bullet? Had his plane, unguided, crashed to the earth? Would he, Bangs, live to?

Buck's hurried thoughts were suddenly checked by a sharp, stinging sensation that began at his side, then seemed to fill him completely. At the same time he realized that his hands no longer hold the steering wheel. He strove to seize it again, but his muscles did not obey. A stupor was on him. The sunlight faded, gave way to a bewildering maze of twinkling stars. His last conscious sensation was that his machine was crashing downward. Then came a long mental blank.

Meantime Blaine was having his own troubles.

The rest of the air fighting had gone eastward, while he was contending with the increased crippling of his planes. Overhead he saw only the now clearing sky. Ahead of him, beyond a rippling stream, lay certain trenches held, he felt sure, by his own side. But could be reach them? Far behind the noise of battle rumbled. Where was Buck? Somehow he had lost sight of his comrade within the last few minutes.

"Buck is a good, bang-up fellow. We ought to go back together."

But his power was waning. Try as he might, the plane was sagging groundward. Only Blaine's skilful efforts kept it from dropping with a crash which he knew would probably be the end of him—Lafe Blaine.

What was that just below him which some scraggy shell-torn timber had kept him from seeing before?

"Looks like a piece of a house," he muttered.

Stoutly he tried to make the small open space around this half ruined hovel. Almost he made, it. But just beyond a crumbling stone wall, that once must have been the enclosure of a tidy yard, the tail of his machine dipped all at once. It struck the wall, causing the heavier bow, weighted with the propellers, the petrol tank and the machinery, to crash downward with force.

The recoil sent Blaine, now at the last physical gasp, plunging forward over the almost perpendicular machine. He struck the earth heavily, and lay there almost insensible, while the vanquished plane fell sideways, striking wall and ground, then, with a last respiration not unlike that of its master, it lay still, a wreck for the time being.

From out the house two skirted figures ran, figures in nurse's attire, with the omnipresent red cross blazoned conspicuously on their white-capped headgear.

"Oh, Andra, Andra!" cried the first to the one following. The last cast a swift glance back inside the cabin. Then she, too, hurried to the prostrate form lying beside the wrecked machine.

Chapter 10
A Quick Convalescence

Two days later. The scene had changed. The Allied front, leaving the rippling stream some two miles or more in the rear, was now showing a convex bend towards the foe instead of a concave hollow, as was the case before the fighting.

The little half-ruined cabin was in decidedly better shape than before. A number of Red tents and temporary wooden shelters had risen if by magic in the small open space around. Trenches stretched eastward, communicating the new trenches now occupied by Americans French, with a sprinkling of British forces.

That the new front was considered as something to be held permanently was further indicated the rapid construction of a new road for automobiles and motor-car traffic along this new line. Even ties, lumber and rails were being piled here and there, as foretokening that one more of the many short lines of railway was now being prepared for use in the near future.

Still further back was another aerodrome, unfenced as yet, but nearly completed. There was one reassuring sign of its ownership and occupancy. As the light winds flared out its folds, so that all who saw might read, there floated out our own national emblem, the Stars and Stripes.

Inside the restored hut lay Buck Bangs on a white cot, while on another reclined the stalwart form of Lafayette

Blaine. Both of these spad pilots, though pale and looking rather the worse for wear, showed such evidence of comfort and bodily ease that one felt sure things must have happened to both. On the lapel of each coat was military decoration, evidently very recently bestowed.

Blaine at last threw down the magazine he was reading and glared at his partner, who moved with more difficulty when he changed his reclining position for one less unbearable.

"What's got into you, Buck?" said Blaine impatiently. "Why don't you go to sleep? Afraid you'll dream of that pretty girl what picked you up?"

"Little good I get dreaming of her, Lafe! But wasn't it queer? Just as soon as you got straight and I was out of danger, off they went-bang! Durn it! They was both here yesterday while the Doe and Sawbones were at work. My, how that girl could smile—and exclaim!"

"That was one thing she could do, Buck." Blaine grinned. "All her exclaiming was in good Yankee English—real United States."

"And what have we got waiting on us now? Ugh!" Buck made a painful face, but whether caused by his thought or by having to change his position again was not at first apparent.

A middle-aged, rather homely, yet kindly nurse entered and puttered round them both. At last she inquired in rather lame English:

"Will *Monseurs*, so lately promoted for their gallantry—will they have anything more? I shall be delight to —"

"No, no, Madame," broke in Buck, while Blaine furtively grinned. "We are doing finely-finely—ouch!"

"Ees zat anew pain?" The elderly nurse was at once by his side. "We must rest quiet, mon enfant. Quiet for joost one day more. Then you will be moved to our nearest base—"

"Say, Madame!" Buck was interrupting eagerly, "what has become of the girls that were here yesterday?"

"Ah-h! Yes, yes! They are grand Mesdemoiselles—both. Reech! La, la! I hear their father owns r-railroads in your

164

countree. *Oui!* Yiss, yiss, all right. Zere! I am learning ze language. It cooms easy—*adieu!*" And she vanished through the door.

"What do you think of that, Lafe? Why were those two young girls, both Red Cross apprentices, why were they left here alone? Don't they know the Boches would rather bomb a hospital than eat *wienerwurst* for lunch? And then as soon as the place became really safe, off they go; but where?"

"Say, Buck, you make me tired! Hush up! I guess we'll meet up with them some day soon. If we don't—what's the odds?"

"And their daddy—so this blessed old mollycoddle says—owns real United States railroads. Makes me sick! But—say, Lafe! Wasn't that youngest one a beaut? If ever I get a furlough, I'm going to look her up."

"And be a fool for your pains! Look here, you do have sense enough to put up a good fight in the air. But on the ground, the real earth, you're becoming a fool."

But Buck rolled, and grumbled, and so wore himself out fretting that on the next day it was decided to send them both to the base hospital for a week, which was duly done.

Three days more and Blaine, now an ensign, besides having his French decoration) had so nearly regained his strength that he no longer lay on a cot, but sat and walked about, a convalescent.

Buck Bangs, now a sergeant, still fretted and grumbled, improving more slowly. The new stripes on his arm cheered him somewhat, yet he eagerly eyed each group of visitors who strolled through the wards, the reading rooms, and other parts of the big base hospital where the two were convalescing. But, so far, his longings were ungratified.

A few hundred yards further back, on the edge of a French village that now quartered a brigade of our Sammies, was the new aerodrome where (quite a number of Uncle Sam's new aviators were on duty, day and night. Most of those we have met before were there, all except poor Finzer and a few others that had fallen in the various raids that had taken place from time to time. There was Erwin, now a corporal; Lex Brodno, His American Pole, and others . Byers was in charge, with Anson and one or two other British aviators detailed to help the new American airmen get into thorough shape and training.

This recent transfer from the other station had taken place while Blaine and Bangs were absent raiding and subsequently in the hospital. Bauer, the fellow who had made the signal to the enemy the night that raid started, had been tried by court-martial and was to have been shot but on the night before the intended execution he managed to escape, probably by connivance of somebody. It was afterward heard that he had gotten back to Germany by some hook or crook. Would he ever pay the penalty he had so richly deserved? That remains yet to be seen.

On the day when Byers himself escorted Blaine and Bangs from the hospital to the aviation camp, there were many visitors. Amid the cordial welcomes given them by their old comrades and also many new ones, Buck anxiously scanned each group of visitors as they passed. Lafe joked him about this.

"Why, you poor stiff," said the new ensign, "where are you looking? What's wrong, anyhow? Gee! Isn't it jolly to be back among the boys—well, well!"

Blaine interrupted himself when Buck, his eyes roving, suddenly espied two young women, garbed as Red Cross nurses—novitiates—wandering amid the new hangars in which were a score or more of the American machines. Straightway Buck had bolted.

Blaine, following him with his eyes, saw Buck doff his aviator's cap as he reached the group that also included an elderly man and lady, and another matronly form which was easily recognized by many as the head nurse in charge of the new Red Cross stations within the American sector.

"Durn me if he isn't shaking hands with those girls!" soliloquized Lafe. "The cheek of him! If he wasn't such a mighty good fellow, I'd call him down!"

But Blaine was a pretty good chap himself. He and Erwin had come together and were exchanging cordial small talk concerning what had happened to each recently, when he again saw Buck with these visitors strolling leisurely by towards the nearest landing stage. Towards this place a pair of swift scouts were making, on their return from the German front somewhere east.

"Know those folks?" he idly queried of Orris, now a corporal.

"Bet your life! Say, Lafe, who doesn't know of Senator Knute Walsen of Idaho? He's a big man, over here to supervise our rail transportation in France. See those two Red Cross girls? They're his daughters. Taking courses in nursing, I hear, and right at the front too. Wouldn't that get you? Who is that showing them round?"

"That is Buck Bangs, from Butte, Montana—Our old Buck! What d'ye think of that, bo?"

"He seems quite intimate with 'em, don't he? Where'd he meet up with that crowd, Lafe?"

"Well, he and I sort o' dropped in on the girls just before we were in the relief station. Remember, don't you? It was while we were returning home from that raid where poor Finzer got his."

"Don't say! Yes, of course, we've all heard how you and Buck piloted our fellows after you two had been out all night. Had a hell of a time—didn't you?" Suddenly Erwin looked his amazement. "Look here, Lafe. Honest Injun! Were those two daughters of old Walsen in that hut when you and Bangs just managed to make your landing there? Whoopee!"

Blaine had nodded, then looked after the receding group half regretfully. Orris gripped the Ensign's arm, and began telling things.

"They must be plucky girls, all right. It so happened that the older nurse—the one you and I saw later—had gone away with a desperately wounded man in an ambulance to the next base. After you and Buck landed, you were both bad off, he worse than you. Well, sir, the Boches shelled that hut before any one got back, and before our boys had driven the Boches clear off. What do you reckon those two girls did? They didn't holler: nary a squeal! But they stuck to you two and to business, and nursed you both, so that by the time aid arrived, you were all pretty comfortable. Some girls, those two! I hear that the younger, Miss Andra Walsen, is going to remain. Maybe they both are. And as for money, there's wads of it in the family, believe me! No wonder Bucky is bucking up to 'em a bit!"

After this lengthy exordium, Orris discreetly, changed the subject by wanting to know when he and Buck would be assigned again to duty.

"I'm ready right now. Whether Buck is or not I can't say. As for me, I've got the old flying fever, big and hot. I suppose it rests with Byers."

Later on as the group whom they had been discussing approached, Blaine and his friend were introduced. Andra, it was plain to see, had ready given poor Buck a deal to think about later on. She was handsome, dark-eyed, light-haired with a peachy complexion—a combination hard indeed for a susceptible youth to resist. Avella, her sister, blue-eyed, dark-haired, a year older than her sister, was equally fascinating, yet in a different way.

Both were kindly, earnest, in love with their new work, and ready to go anywhere or do anything that would serve the good cause.

As a matter of course, when Erwin excused himself on plea of other business and the Senator, looking at his watch, found he had an appointment with Byers, the four young people were left alone. By couples they strolled through the aerodrome, inspecting this, commenting on that, while other fliers regarded the boys with more or less envy.

After a while several specks were seen in the eastern sky that approached rather more rapidly than was usual with friendly planes at such time of day. Blaine had his glasses out, while listening to the comments of the girls on the difficulties they bad in bringing both boys into that hut and dressing their wounds.

"We had to go for water," said Avella.

"You see we hadn't been there but a day or so. I went, and nearly got lost among the old shell craters before I got to the spring that was an awful distance off. It was dark, and so smoky! I was afraid something might happen while I was away."

"You sure were mighty good to us," remarked Blaine. "What luck! To come way over here and be saved by two lovely girls right from our own part of the world. Can you beat it, Buck?"

"Don't want to beat it! Say, you ladies are our own kind of folks. I'll be homesick when you two leave."

"Perhaps we won't leave—yet." Avella smiled enigmatically. "Papa is willing for us to stay. At first I was going with him; but he says Andra and I would need each other to keep from getting homesick."

"Look, look!" Andra was gazing through Buck's glasses at the approaching planes, which had a strange look as they flew at tremendous speed in V formation. "What if they should not be friendly?"

Just then Blaine closed his own glass for he saw flyers coming on the run.

"Are you two all right?" he called to the boys. "All our best men are off on the daily run over the Boche trenches. I cannot think how these fellows got by. Get down to the hangars, if you feel strong enough. I may have to go up myself. They're making straight for us."

The girls were looking on in wonder, whereat Byers turned to them.

"You better get into the bomb-proofs," he said. "Your father's yonder."

The Senator was seen hurrying from one of the buildings towards them.

Both the aviators, seeing, Erwin and Brodno on the run, joined them and hastened on down to where mechanics were trundling out a number of machines upon the smooth level that was the starting point nearest. With a word to the Senator, Byers followed, while the girls both waved their handkerchiefs. Said Andra to her sister:

"Let us go on down. I want to see them start. Do you think Mr. Bangs is strong enough? Look at him run!"

"I guess he is as strong as Mr. Blaine. But they both really ought to have a few days' leave, don't you think?"

Arrived on the driveway, half a dozen men, all in the leather uniforms with caps and goggles to match, were mounting the machines nearest. Blaine, having donned his rig on the run, as it were, was already in a triplane much like the one he had last used. Turning to the mechanic, he asked:

"It cannot be my own machine, is it?"

"Sure thing!" the man replied. "It was sent to us the day after you got in. We fixed her up, thinking you might need it. Glad you are out so soon, Ensign."

"Thanks for that! I reckon we'll need all we got by the looks of that squad that's coming. They're dropping bombs already."

"Yes, sir," said another mechanic, using his glass. "And right over where you and Sergeant Bangs came down."

CHAPTER 11

The Battles in the Air

In a trice Blaine was rising in the air. The feeling that he had again his old machine was reassuring. It put new life into his nearly restored vitality.

With Buck Bangs a close second and Orris Erwin right behind him, the leading planes spiralled into the air, with the advancing Boches hardly two miles away, their bombs dropping as they flew.

Byers himself was getting into his own plane, a two-seated affair equipped with two machine guns. With him was his own observer, an excellent photographer and airman. The two opposing squadrons were about equal. Dividing into two columns, with Blaine heading one and Captain Byers the other, they bore directly off toward the enemy.

Such a start had the Boches gotten, by somehow missing the Allied planes that were supposed to be picketing the front, that a direct attack was inevitable. Up or down they rose or fell, each plane singling out its opponent, and each manoeuvring for position. It was here that the superior speed and nimbleness of the Allied triplanes was soon apparent.

Byers in his big biplane made straight for the leading plane opposed to him and presently the rattle of machine gun fire interplayed with the whirring sounds of the motors, while the diving, flipping, looping, with all the other air stunts of sky battling, made the scene so interesting to those below that the adjacent bomb-proofs were hardly thought of.

On a small knoll the American senator and his two daughters, glasses in hand, were watching, listening, semi-oblivious as to any possible danger to themselves. Finally a spatter of bullets and shell fragments roused the father to a sense that more than himself might be in the line of fire at any moment.

"This won't do, girls!" he announced in peremptory tones. "Get into that shelter!" pointing at a half underground dug-out near. "Run, run!"

Avella, without lowering her glass, replied:

"In just a minute, papa. See Mr. Blaine! My! What's he doing to that other horrid fellow?"

Blaine was at the instant trying to got on the tail of a big Taube, not unlike the one Blaine and Erwin had captured and used while on an earlier scout, as may be recalled by the reader. What accentuated Blaine's eagerness was the glimpse he caught of that Death's Head Flag, which had also adorned the former captured machine. But the Boche within this one was an adept and so manoeuvred that Blaine, to save himself from an onset from behind, was obliged to try the risky side-loop, much to the surprise of the other. For Blaine, while upside down, was already firing at his opponent, and as he rose was directly on the tail. But to the girls below it looked as if Blaine was already crashing towards the earth. Andra gave a nervous scream. Avella was shocked, of course, but had her glass the next instant upon Buck Bangs, at that moment engaged in a fierce duel with two enemy opponents.

"Look! Look!" called Andra. "He's falling—ah-h-h!" This last word was long drawn out during which, to her intense joy, Blaine had righted himself and was behind and below the other plane. Now she could see the spitting of lire as he plugged bullets and shrapnel into his astonished opponent.

Scarcely did she breathe again before the Taube, its Death's Head Flag collapsing about its staff, was tumbling down, almost over them. At the same time one of the Huns battling with Bangs was hit in the tank by a rain of bullets from Byers' machine which was striving to rise above and behind the foe the captain had singled out for himself.

Down went this one of Buck's opponents in flames. Both planes fell just without the grounds, while the battle above filtered away towards the German front, the invaders evidently having gotten enough. Two other enemy planes were retiring in a crippled condition, all pursued by the Allies, who had so far lost only one machine.

The Senator, seeing little heed paid by his daughters to his commands, was seized by the spirit of the combat and recklessly hurried off towards the nearest wrecked plane that had fallen. The girls, with others, followed.

It was a sad sight. This machine, the wings still burning, lay in a confused huddle over a crushed human body that still gave signs of life. It was the plane that Byers bad sent down in flames.

Aided by men from the aerodrome, they extinguished the fire with a ready hose, the Senator and the girls assisting. Carefully they dragged out a horribly mutilated yet youthful form. A surgeon, with the girls aiding, tried to alleviate the, pain of the dying man. His lips moved.

"What's he trying to say, Vella?" demand the Senator. "You know some German, don't you?"

"Sounds like *'schwein, Schwein!'* Doesn't that mean pigs, papa?"

"It sure does! There, he's talking again!"

The girls listened, but could not understand; while the surgeon, formerly an intern at one of the New York hospitals, smiled pityingly.

"Poor fellow!" he volunteered. "He's not complimentary."

"What's he saying now? Sounds like American—then something else."

"He says, *'Amerikaner*—all swine-pigs,' and a lot more."

They drew back somewhat; but the girls whose sympathy predominated, continued to minister to his needs until the last breath announced that one more Boche had gone to his account.

It was an hour or so before the rest of the squadron again appeared. With them were the scouting planes that had been wished for when the enemy squadron so suddenly appeared. In the fights over the German trenches another of our planes had somehow vanished. No one could say further except that Erwin, the missing pilot, had been seen mounting high up amid a scurry of clouds, with two pursuing Fokkers on his heels.

Blaine and Bangs were in the midst of hearty congratulations from many, including Senator Walsen and his daughters, when the news was brought to them.

They had just alighted and were standing beside their machines. Instantly Blaine turned to Buck, saying:

"You and your machine all right, Buck?"

Andra, at this, regarded Lafe closely.

"I'm O. K. and so is my bully little Nieuport. Say, old man, we've got to go out and see what's gone wrong with that little snipe Orry, eh?"

" Sure thing! Orry is a good fellow. I'm with you."

The next instant Blaine was back in his seat. He turned to the mechanic who had just finished examining the machine.

"Fill up the tank, Bill," he said. "And hand me out a few more sheaves of ammunition. Sure you've got enough, too, Buck?"

"Do you—do you—you don't mean that you two are going up again?" queried Andra, and for an instant Blaine detected something about her that betokened a more than casual interest.

"It's my—it's our duty to go, Miss Walsen," said he, meeting her eyes sympathetically. "Erwin is one of our best men. He's a true spad pilot. Besides that, he and I are great cronies. Buck feels the same way."

"Oh, I—I think I understand." But she spoke with a certain repressed agitation. If Lafe had been less se1f-conscious he would have understood and doubtless felt flattered.

As it was, he turned to Bangs, the Montana lad, now also seated in his pilot's place, with Avella on the other side saying something. He heard Bangs reiterate:

"Oh, sure, Miss Vella! We'll be careful—very careful—you bet! I'm only too anxious to get back with Orry and see more of you two girls. I say, Senator," to the father now looking approvingly on, "this lost pilot is one of our best. He's a turnip—a real joker! We can't go back on him."

"I guess you are right, Mr. Bangs. If you and your friends do return to us, I will see that you all have leave to run back to Paris and at least take dinner with us at our hotel."

By this time the two young nurses were standing back, watching the scene with the frank mien that American girls view something which they regret, yet at the same time admire. Then up came Captain Byers hurriedly, calling out:

"Are you lads going? That's plucky! I was about to dispatch some one. We cannot afford to lose Erwin. He's too valuable, and I know he'd do the same by you!"

"You bet, Captain!" This from Buck as his machine trundled off, propelled by two mechanics until it rose. "That was bully the way you busted that chap in the tank. He might have got me, else."

Blaine was already in the air, with Bangs a close second. A moment later and they were climbing rapidly, so rapidly that soon they looked like two great birds winging their way over the Allied front and across No-Man's-Land into the dark beyond. Blaine's observer, Stanley, was also in his seat behind.

When the two girls finally reached their quarters that night at the small inn in the adjacent village they were both dispirited. The Senator was writing letters while the girls were preparing for the evening meal.

"Funny, isn't it, how we seem to be interested in those lads?" said Andra. "I think that young Blaine is just splendid."

"He is no better than Mr. Bangs." This from Avella. "Just think, Buck is from Butte! Why, that is right next door to us in Idaho."

Then they both sighed, looked queerly at each other and finally embraced and kissed. If both were somewhat smitten over the looks and conduct of these aviators, acquaintances of only a few days, certainly their stately father as yet could hardly suspect.

After the evening meal was over, they cunningly tried to persuade him to go with them down to the aerodrome to see if anything had occurred there. Probably the boys had not yet returned. The Senator doubted if they had.

"Look here, girls," said be, after being told that he was needed as an escort, "why are you so interested? They'll come back all right. And I am busy."

"Well, papa, said Avella, "we'd feel better to go down and inquire."

"Yes, daddy dear! You must go with us, please!"

The upshot of all this was as usual. The Senator went.

At the station they found Captain Byers returning from an observation post where he had been scanning the eastern heavens in a last effort to discern something of the absent planes that had long since vanished over No-Man's-Land into the unknown void beyond, which was enemy country.

"I am afraid for those lads," said he to the Senator after greeting all three. "They are both too risky at times, and they were much stirred up over Erwin's long absence. Great friends they were, too."

The Senator and the girls expressed concern. Especially so was it with the sisters, both of whom grew pale as they listened. Perhaps they were pleased that owing to the darkness this manifestation of inward concern was hidden from the others. They quietly pressed each other's hands.

Just then an orderly came up on the run, his night glasses in hand.

"Oh, Captain," said he, "there's a plane returning. I couldn't make it out clearly. It sags a bit is if it was crippled, sir."

"Wait for me, Senator," called Byers, starting out almost on the run, his night glasses again out. The orderly followed rapidly.

"Let us follow them, father," urged Andra, while Avella

tugged at her sister's arm, sure that the Senator would go too. "Come on, papa."

Both girls were off, while the Senator came after, though at a slower pace.

Reaching the observation post—merely a platform erected on the highest elevation near by, they saw the captain and the orderly both scanning the eastern skies through their night glasses, instruments of the latest design. To the girls' nothing was as yet was visible but the stars now shining dimly through a thin haze that hung over h landscape.

"Let us go up. Papa will follow." This from Andra as they climbed the steps to the little platform where the two aviators were scanning the upper air.

From the disjointed remarks of the airmen the realized that something was in sight, yet hardly visible to the naked eye. At last, however, came a gasp from one of the girls who pointed eagerly to the other.

"Don't you see it?" exclaimed Andra. "Where are your eyes? My! It's sagging downward. I wonder —'

Here Avella interrupted with a slight scream as she too, caught sight of a faint, filmy something that was teetering slowly down, but not in straight lines as is usual when planes are descending in the regular methods employed by aviators when striving to reach a certain landing.

"What is the matter with it?" queried Andra to any one within hearing.

"That you, ladies?" Byers turned suddenly, then his eyes sought his glass again. "Why, it is quite evident that the machine is a Fokker and disabled. He'll make it all right, I guess."

"That is a German machine, isn't it?" asked Avella anxiously.

"Mightn't it be a hostile one?" queried Andra.

"The plane is of hostile make, Miss Walsen, but the chap inside is one of us, you may be sure. There! I fear he is going to drop."

Byers, followed by the orderly, was already running down

the steps, almost colliding with the Senator who arrived at this moment. After the two aviators hurried the girls, meeting their father, and telling him what was occurring.

"And Captain Byers said that airman was about to drop— or fall out; I don't know which." This from Andra. "Let us hurry after them, father, and see what has happened."

Senator Walsen, evidently used to these sudden whims on the part of his daughters, turned and followed them, still in pursuit of the captain. If he objurgated the haste, he did it silently.

By the time the girls caught up with Byers, what had been a trim airplane came thumping to the ground not more than two hundred yards off in an unused corner of the big enclosure, its wings a mere mass of tattered rags, its body riddled by many perforations of machine gun bullets, fragments of shrapnel and so on. It was a marvel how it had stayed up for so long, but it happened that neither the engine nor petrol tank were vitally harmed.

Still lashed to his seat, his arms hanging loosely, his head resting on the rim of the small manhole, was the pilot, to all appearances lifeless or else in a swoon. It was Stanley, Blaine's observation man.

CHAPTER 12

The Adventures of Erwin

In the meantime, what had become of the two adventurous planes with their occupants that had so blithely started out in search of the still missing pilot and friend? Whither had their search carried them? How was it that of the three who went forth only one had come back, perhaps lifeless or barely alive, and in a German machine!

Verily in this new warfare of the air strange are the daily happenings on that fated West Front; nor can anybody foretell what stranger things may happen than have happened before, even to the best pilots of them all.

During the air fighting when the Boches were sent back in retreat, with some of their best planes missing, Erwin, after sending one already half crippled Fokker crashing to earth, took after another German. This last was a huge biplane manned by two men, one of whom lay collapsed in his seat. The remaining pilot seemed bewildered. Already the plane had received various punctures, though not sufficient to prevent further flying.

"No use to let that chap get away," reflected Orris. "He's lost his observer, and his wings are in bad shape. Our fellows can attend to the rest of these Boches. We've got 'em whipped anyway."

Up, up went the German, with Erwin following, trying to circle round into position to use his machine gun. But this was not easy. The biplane, though crippled, was of such power and speed that it easily kept well ahead of its pursuer who was yet far below. In fact, when an altitude of several thousand feet was attained, the greater buoyancy of the air at this stage was an aid to the half defeated foe. His vast spread of double wings made it difficult for Orris, with his greater motor power and reduced spread of planes, to much more than neutralize their relative positions.

Straight into the northeast fled the German. After him came Erwin, still below and striving to get onto his adversary's tail. But despite all he could do, it failed to bring him within the proper distance for direct attack.

"That is be up to now?" wondered the youth, for the Boche was half rising in his seat, as if trying to lift something behind. "Hullo! Blame me if he ain't trying to oust his dead mate!"

This was exactly what the Boche pilot was trying to do. But for some reason, not at first apparent, the man had difficulties. At last, by letting go with both hands of wheel and controls, half turning in his seat, Erwin saw him lift up the body of the observer and attempt to fling it overboard. But even that was hindered for a moment, and in a way that filled the watchful American with horror and disgust.

Already the seemingly inanimate body was sliding over the sloping side of the car, when Orris saw a hand stretch forth, seize the pilot's extended arm and hang thus, half dangling over the side, the legs kicking feebly.

"Why, his mate's alive!" almost shouted the American, more shaken by this exhibition than anything that had hitherto happened to him in his short but risky campaign along the West Front.

"Hey, there! You beast—you villain!" Almost insanely Erwin was shouting, for he was convulsed by a fury that made him for the time being oblivious to the fact that he was too far away to be heard by any one but himself.

For another instant the half alive man hung on, then was shaken loose. Down he came, passing rather close to the scouting pursuer, his arms and legs still working convulsively, and so on down to his inevitable fate. By this time, and while Erwin was recovering, the big biplane had recovered and was shooting eastward as before though with accelerated speed, being now relieved of much of its former dead weight.

Still grinding his teeth, Orris shot after the foe, determined more than ever to overtake and have it out with the inhuman beast, now alone in his flight to safety but a mile ahead.

All thought of immediate return to his own lines was lost, at least until he could wreak vengeance on the man who had just shown such inhumanity towards his own comrade and countryman.

"Curse him!" still objurgated the youth. "It would be bad enough if it was a foe—one of us that was aboard that cursed craft!" Orris expelled a deep breath, while he put on all the power his speedy plane would stand. "I'll get him even if the Boches got me!"

From the course followed by the biplane Erwin knew that he was already well to the northward of the point of his own return, provided he was able to make the trip back in safety. Also it was clear that they were now well over the rear German trenches and not very far from where Belgian territory bordered on that part of northern France—now so long held by the foe.

So swift and fast did Erwin go that the transient aid afforded by casting over the still living observer was soon more than neutralized. The boy was almost within easy range.

"Just a little further and I'll get him." So ran Erwin's thought. "But I mustn't waste ammunition. There's no knowing when or where I'll need all I've got. Curse that beast! He shall die or I'll know the reason why, even if I get into a narrow squeeze myself."

At last he felt that he might begin. He was on the tail of the biplane, though underneath. To his gratification he also saw that in nimble activity he was now the superior. And in close fighting it is the nimble, ducking, dodging, twisting machine that usually has certain advantage.

Pointing upward, he began to rain bullets and shrapnel into the fleeing German, his Lewis gun working automatically, and with such precision that the German shot off at right angles, dived, and strove to come up underneath his assailant. But he was too slow. After the dive, as the biplane came up in reverse position Erwin, prepared for this, half wheeled, and shot obliquely downward, pointed straight at his adversary. While he darted at a two-mile-a-minute pace, the deadly Lewis again began vomiting its flaming death straight at the man seated amidships, who was frantically trying to train his own gun on the advancing foe.

On came the scouting plane from five hundred yards to less than two hundred, almost while one drew an average breath. Evidently the German misunderstood. He thought that the now reckless foe, casting discretion to the wind, was bent upon something desperate. But—what? Again and again he tried to train his own gun on the American, but the latter kept edging just out of range, while at the same time he drew near, nearer.

At last, when within fifty yards, Erwin let him have it. While his Lewis was spitting forth a continuous fire, by some method not at once comprehended by the other, Erwin ranged alongside, still at a distance where he was free from air suction, and literally riddled that big plane with holes. After a spattering fire that did no harm, the German abandoned the gun and strove to nosedive, always a rather risky proceeding in such a big plane when haste is apt to neutralize efficiency.

Instead of presenting a slanting pair of wings, the big machine was tipped in such a way as to present for a minute, its whole under side to Erwin's view.

It was the critical moment. With feet on controls, and one hand on the wheel, the lad managed to pour a continuous volley of those leaden hailstones squarely into the entrails of the foe. Then up he climbed, at almost lightning speed, and as he came to dancing level off the German's tail, out from the sagging biplane pitched another human body, this time not the murdered, but the murderer.

"Good riddance!" almost gasped Erwin. "He's gone to hell, where he and his like belong! But—what's this? Glory! His tank is busted; his plane goes down with him and on fire!"

Erwin was correct. The biplane's tank—always in danger in fights like this—had been badly punctured by the same hail of Lewis bullets that had also hit the German, just as his plane got out of control. Instantly the flames burst forth as the big airship plunged downward, only a little behind the falling body of its pilot.

With great effort—for the excitement had weakened the lad—did Erwin bring his scouting plane to an easier level and gait. Then he looked down.

Already both burning biplane and falling pilot had vanished. Far below, the earth was only faintly visible through the mantling haze that now permeated the lower atmosphere. All directions looked alike. The air was comparatively still, and only the far distant rumble of artillery, seldom absent along that front, was audible. It sounded not unlike intermittent thunder. What to do next? Which way should he go? For the first time since starting he felt for his compass. It was gone.

"What'll I do now?" he asked himself.

"Where is the sun? I suppose all the boys that started when I did must have gone back long ago. The time must be at least mid-afternoon." The mists below evidently were rising and thickening. The boy hated to acknowledge to himself that he must be lost, but it looked that way. Cautiously he descended to lower levels but the landscape thus opaquely revealed showed but little that was definite. Lower still he flew. As the earth grew more and more distinct its strangeness did not diminish.

Though it was risky, he went lower still, until the tops of trees, the signs of half ruined houses began to appear. But nothing familiar was in sight. About this time, with day waning and his anxiety growing, Erwin was at last rewarded by glimpse of the sinking sun, seen hazily through a canopy of clouds. There was no mistaking that it was the sun and Orris found that he must have flown wrongly ever since he had put the Boche biplane out of commission. Already he was heading westward when from below there came a series of sharp reports from artillery evidently close by.

"Surely they cannot be shelling our trenches from way back here. I must be far behind the enemy lines—much too far to suit me. Ah, I what's that?"

That was an unmistakable whistle of bullets too close to be comfortable. At least one or two perforated his wings. Then Erwin pointed higher at the same time trying to keep his sense of direction, imparted by a momentary sight of the western sun. More gun shots: still more whistling of balls, and all too close to be comforting.

Up, up he went, veering more to the west. All at once came other gunshots, this time in an extended roar from an area covering perhaps a mile in extent.

"The Archies are getting too familiar," he grumbled. "I must put on more speed. Won't do for me to fail to return."

About that time a breeze sprang up from the east and the skies cleared through a narrow Vista, showing a war-scarred belt of country below with a small town ahead; that is, toward the west. But before he had time to consider this, he saw two airplanes rising from the main street of the little town, while the detonations of the Archies grew into a continuous roar.

"Guess they think they've cornered me," he thought, "but I'll give them a race at least. If I have to, I'll fight."

While reflecting, his machine was still rising rapidly, with the two Boche planes in pursuit.

"They won't catch me unless I'm crippled by those pesky Archies."

Even while he thought, a stray fragment of shell penetrated the fuselage of the triplane and, striking one of the propeller shafts, so bent it that the lightning-like blades began to revolve more slowly, despite all his efforts to increase his motor power.

For the first time Erwin became seriously alarmed. Try as

he might, he was in no position to stop to make repairs, nor could he descend with safety. Apparently the only thing for him to do was to speed up as best he could, try to avoid this pursuit and, if it came to close quarters, put up the best fight possible under the circumstances.

This, of course, he did. But the sight of their own planes pursuing, and at the same time signalling to their friends below, caused Erwin at once to become the target for a continuous line of Archies, extending from the front line German trenches way back to the unknown distances in their rear.

When the pursuing planes drew nearer, the shelling from below grew less, while the condition of his own plane was such as to cause alarm. He knew that he was cornered. Cornered, too, in a way seldom happening to the birdmen who became temporarily lost in a raid. He eyed the two nearing scout planes with no little aversion. Not only was his machine going at less speed, despite his efforts, but the difficulty in steering was greater. Apparently if would only obey the rudder slowly, no matter how hard he tried to "get a move on her." As for wheeling, volplaning, spiralling or doing anything that occasioned quick action on his part with rudder or planes, he was nearly helpless.

Meantime the pursuing planes, both Fokker scouting machines, drew still nearer and began to use their machine guns. The balls pattered all about; but as yet neither he nor his plane was hit. He was zigzagging, mounting, spiralling, but all in a much slower fashion than he had been used to do with this same plane before.

"What's the use?" he groaned. "I can't get back at them, even if I am running away. It's got to come. What's the odds? I'll turn and give them one good try for their game, anyhow."

He was already turning in his lame evolutions when something like a big shadow darkened the air for an instant overhead. It passed. Then back came the shadow again, and a voice was megaphoning, not from below or in the rear but from right overhead. It said:

"Hey, you, Orry! You're crippled! I can see that. But why don't you come up higher? Get a move on!"

Erwin knew that voice. It was like a trumpet call to the lad. Fiercely be seized his own megaphone and shouted back, while with one hand and his feet he kept his own flier still going.

"Yes? I'm crippled but all right. I can't rise except slowly. Better go while the going's good! Too many Archies below!"

While Orris was shouting, another shadow passed overhead. It was Buck Bangs in his Nieuport. For hours they had been scouring the eastern air-zone in a vain search for Erwin, when the sudden roaring of the Archies turned them in this direction. While Orris was turning, trying also to rise, he saw as he faced to the rear that two planes instead of one were now charging the enemy. These had for a minute or more been directing their machine gun fire upon the new arrivals. Erwin had heard the noise of them, and wondered why he was not hit again. This was the reason.

"Great boys, they are," he said to himself.

"But I hope looking for me has not led them where we all don't want to go," meaning the prison camps of the Huns, from which had oozed stories of starvation and cruelty that were more than bad enough. "Considering how I'm fixed, I'll lay low down here and watch my chance to help. That other chap must be Bangs. Well, those two have got nerve anyhow!"

CHAPTER 13

At the Ruined Chateau

Having found the man they were searching for and in so perilous a situation, neither Blaine nor Bangs wasted time. If Erwin was crippled, so much the greater reason for them to relieve him. Only by direct attack could this be accomplished, if at all. Though the Archies were now roaring more than ever, Blaine and his observer, both machine guns pointed f or instant action, started straight at the pursuing planes. Buck was with him at a convenient distance. Instantly the rattle of their guns pattered out in the air as a fusillade of bullets was showered at the foe.

The determined manoeuvres of the new arrivals evidently daunted the Huns. One of them immediately turned tail. The other tried to do so but was intercepted by Blaine who, making an absolutely nervy side-loop, came up under the Fokker and began again discharging a deadly rain of bullets.

But one source of refuge was left the German. Up, up he climbed. Being cut off from retreat towards his own lines, he struck straight across towards No-Man's-Land with the big biplane full pursuit and still firing.

Meantime Bangs took after the other, bringing it down under a detached fire from the Archies who were naturally more cautious now in firing, owing to the fear of hitting one of their own planes. Still they found chances to pepper the little Nieuport in which Bangs was darting to and fro like a hawk after a chicken. But before the Fokker was sent down, Buck knew that his own wings were seriously perforated. As yet his fuselage and tank, his engine and machinery were unhurt.

Without waiting to note the fate of his opponent, Bangs turned nimbly and struck out westward, following the crippled scout wherein was the man they had set out to find and rescue.

"I'll stick by Orry," was Buck's conclusion. "I guess Blaine and Stanley can take care of that other chap. I wonder where the rest of the Huns are. We are in the rear lines and there should be more Fokkers or Taubes around."

This query was soon answered. Ranging alongside Erwin, but not too near, Buck megaphoned as follows:

"How you getting on anyhow? Had a hell of a time findin' you. Didn't find you any too soon, eh?"

Erwin's replies were unimportant except that he was so crippled that he must get back to the base, or at least alight somewhere soon or he, would not be able to fly at all.

"Bent piston rods," he also phoned. "And I'm afraid my main propeller shaft has gone wrong somehow."

"All right," returned Bangs. "I'll stick with you. Hullo! What's the matter with Blaine and his man?"

At this juncture the big biplane that had been pursuing the Fokker suddenly ducked, dove far beneath his adversary and came up on the opposing side, at the same time peppering the Hun with machine gun explosive bullets.

The Fokker almost stopped and appeared to tremble. Both Bangs and Erwin saw that some serious internal injury had occurred. The German was furiously at work within his manhole, leaving the plane much to its own devices.

So patent was this that Buck, who was nearest, shot upward and let drive at the Hun from below. But instead of giving heed to this new attack, the Hun now recovered, shot off to the right and began climbing rapidly. Bangs, in accord with his resolve to stick to Erwin, did not follow, but Blaine did, at the same time megaphoning to both Buck and Orris as follows:

"I've been up higher than you fellows. There's a number of planes off in the sou'west. Gettin' so dark could hardly tell 'em apart. Better stick together and watch out!"

Though the Archies were now quite out of range, night was so near at hand that this seemed good policy. Blaine now added:

"I'm goin' to give that Fokker another round. Be back with you in a minute." Then on he went after the German.

What ensued was rather puzzling to both Bangs and Erwin. Blaine was now evidently faster than the German, whose machine had apparently sustained some internal injury. They saw the biplane close in on the Hun amid a rapid fire of bullets from each at the other.

All at once the Hun began sidling irregularly towards the earth. By this time both the others, having risen somewhat, caught glimpses through their field glasses of a number of nearing planes winging from the west. Below, as far as could be seen, stretched No-Man's-Land. Behind was a growing blackness that denoted approaching night. To both Bangs' and Erwin's astonishment, the biplane, instead of returning, was pointing downward after the crippled Fokker.

Then from the north whirled a sea-fog that presently enveloped all, obliterating what remained of light, hiding even Blaine and the adversary he had pursued. It was strange, mysterious.

Erwin, who was lower than the others, here saw the crumbling walls and towers of what had once been an old baronial chateau. Near this the biplane had landed. No sign just then of the Fokker, though that must have descended also, for the machine or the man in it was undoubtedly injured. Erwin grabbed his megaphone, shouting up at Buck hovering near, "I'm going down. Blaine's already landed. Come on!"

But for some reason Bangs declined. Being higher up, he had detected signs of those other planes invisible to those below.

"Go on down," he shouted. "I want to do a little scouting." And off he flew, determined all at once to find out who and what might be approaching. But his purpose was defeated by the onrush of the fog, that thickened still more, while those landed below were equally invisible to Buck.

However having a general idea as to the direction best for him to take, he turned that way after recklessly feeling out in vain for further sight of the approaching squadron. Here we will leave him for the present.

When Erwin at last brought his plane down beside the half ruined chateau, he found both Stanley and Blaine stooping over a prostrate form soon identified as that of the German aviator. Near by was the Fokker, somewhat disabled, but not in such bad condition. The man himself had just expired.

"What do you think that chap asked us to do," said Blaine, regarding the dead man solemnly. "It sort of mellowed me towards him, after His father and mother live in Chicago, worked for some meat packers, and his dad is making some money there. When he found that the bullets that had hit him as well as his machine weren't goin' to let him live much longer, he asked if either of us got back to our lines, to write tell his mother. He gave me the name and I put it down in my pocket pad book. He talked in good English and altogether seemed quite like some of our home folks. He got into aviation over here and liked it. But he's out of all that now and to make him feel better both Stan and I promised to do as he wished.

"He said his machine was all right; and if anything was the matter with ours we might fix up his and make a get-away. Course there ain't nothin' much the matter with mine, though yours may be crippled—hullo! What's that?"

The loud report of an exploding bomb sounded as it fell not far away. Instantly they scattered for such shelter as was obtainable. Other bombs fell and for a few minutes the scene was indescribable. They saw from the shelter both their own machines shattered too badly for further immediate use, though the Fokker remained untouched, it being some distance off and partially under the protecting shadow of a half ruined arch of the chateau that overhung the main approach.

Also they heard the whirring swish of the passing squadron as it circled over the buildings. It afterwards appeared that the chateau owner was for some reason specially obnoxious to the Germans in Belgium. At last the bombing apparently ceased, but even this was deceptive. Both Blaine and Erwin, followed at a little distance by Stanley, ran out to look into the damage done to their machines. In the darkness this was slow work. A fire was lighted, and while still examining the wrecks another whirring overhead sounded.

Stanley discreetly dodged under another projecting abutment, when down dropped another bomb, probably thrown at a venture from some scattering member of the squad that had just passed. From his shelter Stanley was horrified to see both Blaine and Erwin, who were near the fire, thrown violently down as the bomb burst appallingly near where they were crouched. They; did not rise again.

Without waiting to see if other bombs might fall, the observer ran forward in great perturbation. Both aviators lay apparently senseless. From Blaine's head blood was flowing from a flesh wound somewhere up under his thick mop of short curly hair. His pulse, however, was beating lively.

As for Erwin, no visible wounds were apparent, yet he lay there deathly pale while some of his clothing had been torn by fragments of the exploding bomb.

Of Buck Bangs there was no sign.

Deeply depressed, for he was very young and impressionable, Stanley, regardless of his own safety, punched up the fire and from his own and his comrades' kits procured such remedies as aviators carry for just such emergencies. In the dark he hunted for water but found none. From a flask of good French brandy he managed to pour a spoonful or so down each throat, taking a swallow himself, for he felt he sorely needed it.

Poor old Blaine never stirred. Erwin at last shivered slightly.

"Isn't this a deuce of a fix?" he sighed at length. "Where are we? For all I know, Blaines may be dead. Here, feeling again of

Lafe's pulse, its steady beat somewhat reassured Stanley. "How about Orris?"

If anything, Erwin's pulse was coming back. The brandy had restored such vitality to the lad that his arteries were again sending the life-giving fluid upon its unceasing task.

"What can have become of Buck?"

Stanley replenished the fire with stray fuel, for he knew that it would be a signal to Bangs and perhaps to the enemy; but as to the last he hoped not, amid that chilly darkness and night fog.

Here a slight noise from his rear caused Stanley to wheel in his tracks and stare stupidly at a dim figure under the shadow of a portico in front of the basement of the main edifice, which was, in fact, about the only part of that vast group of buildings that seemed unharmed.

"Who are you? What brought you here?" came an unmistakably feminine voice.

More wonderful still, the language was English—good English, too. Was there not also an American twang about the tone and accent? Stanley could have pinched himself, had he thought of it. But so surprised was he that he seemed actually paralyzed, when an unmistakably girlish figure emerged more into the light.

Still the young observer stared, hardly noticed that another older form had made a dim appearance. It, too, wore skirts, though rather raged and soiled. The girl's habiliments also evinced that her recent abode had not been where style and cleanliness were at all dominant.

"You—you are not Germans?" This tremulously from the girl. "You understand me, don't you?"

"Yes, ma am," Stanley almost stuttered.

"Y-you s-see—I'm some surprised—"

"Some surprised!" The girl was smiling hopefully. "That sounds like good old United States talk."

"We heard so much noise overhead, then some nasty bombs exploding. So Brenda and I have lain hidden in the cellars for—for hours. Haven't we, Brenda? The dim form in the rear nodded emphatically. "But who are you?"

Here she caught sight of the ruined planes and the prostrate forms of Blaine and Erwin, with also the more distant figure of the dead German.

"Oh—oh!" She clasped her hands. "How dreadful! What can we do? May we not help? Are they all dead?"

The girl was genuinely aroused, so much so that her natural horror of the strained situation was lost in genuine concern. Stanley briefly explained the series of incidents that had preceded the present situation, at the same time pointing at the dead German aviator, and concluding with:

"The poor chap used to live in Chicago. Before he died he gave us his parents' address there. He spoke good English."

"Why, Chicago is where I hail from," said the girl. "Good old Windy City! I wish I was there now, although I have been over here many months."

Meantime Brenda, with the ready adaptability of Belgian women, had been examining the persons of the two still insensible aviators. All at once she rose up, saying to her mistress:

"Pardon, miss." This in her own Flemish tongue. "We must move these Americans to our under ground rooms. They will recover, but they need attention."

"You are sure right, Miss—Miss—" Stanley hesitated, but the girl paid no heed. "We don't want to inconvenience you, but something will have to be done right away."

With the able assistance of Brenda, while the girl went ahead carrying a small lamp that had been produced as if by magic from somewhere—possibility by Brenda—they picked up poor Erwin and followed. Down some half ruined stone steps they went, then through a long passage, then down more steps to a half open door.

Once inside, Stanley saw he was in quite a sizeable room, with two beds, one large, the other a mere cot. The girl led the way to the large bed, and there they laid the still swooning man who gave a slight groan as he was deftly covered by the girl who murmured as if to herself:

"Poor fellow, he has suffered!"

Already Stanley was leaving, saying:

"We must get Blaine down here quickly. He is in a bad way, I fear."

Seizing the lamp, the girl hurried after. On reaching the other stricken aviator, what was their surprise to find him leaning on one elbow, trying to rise, but vainly.

"Wha—what's the matter? Where am I?"

"You're with friends, old boy," soothed Stanley, seizing Blaine's arms, while Brenda took up the lower limbs. With the wounded man muttering aimlessly, again they wended their way to the lower chamber, evidently used by the girl and Brenda as a temporary sleeping place.

With deft efficiency the girl had snatched up Stanley's kit of dressings and other medical paraphernalia and hurried on ahead with the lamp. In a trice they had placed him on the cot. Immediately the two women were busy with these things and some stored aids of their own, dressing the bruises on both the boys and applying restoratives, so that in a short time both were awake, sensible, and staring with grateful wonder at these two women—angels of mercy—and the strange yet comfortable surroundings.

Mutual explanations had already begun when whirring, semi-thunderous noises again were heard. Stanley was instantly on the alert.

"All of you remain quiet while I slip up and see what is on," he said, flinging back: "If your light is apt to shine through any hole or opening, better douse it or hang up covers. Make no noises until you hear from me." He was off, but not before the girl called to him:

"Be very careful, sir! We cannot spare you—yet."

"No, we can't, ma'am," remarked Blaine from the cot where he now sat upright with a bandaged head.

"Indeed, Sir," said the girl almost wistfully, "we cannot

spare any of you. Just think, we have been here a week, and with more or less bombing going on each day and sometimes at night."

"May I ask, mademoiselle—" began Blaine.

"Just plain Miss," interrupted the girl. "Miss Daskam from Chicago!"

"Well, well!" Blaine was smilingly openly now. "That surely sounds homelike! Well, we're all Americans too. We were on an air raid and had a good deal of mixed luck. Blaine's my name; that's Erwin over there," pointing at the cot where Orris was grinning and smiling. "The chap who went out just now is Stanley. He is my observer. But our machine is smashed now and how we will all get back is more than I know. Eh, Orry?"

"Looks that way. But what's the use of worrying while we are in such charming company? I'm all right."

And to prove it Erwin stepped out on the floor, a little teetery perhaps, but once more himself. He made a not ungraceful bow.

"May I ask, Miss Daskam, how you happened to get cornered down here in this poor old chateau? It must have been a grand place once—but now!" He shrugged slightly, regarding Miss Daskam sympathizingly.

"The wife of the owner of this place is my sister. I came over as a member of the Belgian Red Cross. Both my sister and her husband are, or were, at headquarters when I left the Belgian lines. I had a permit to visit his chateau; for in the days before I came over here I had left there certain papers most important to them both. I wanted to see the place and I had a friend that was chummy with the Boches in Brussels. He had forwarded me a pass. So I insisted on taking Brenda along and trying it alone. You know western girls are not much afraid of things."

"Well, you were plucky enough, anyhow, interposed Erwin and Blaine nodded.

"Up to that time, after the chateau had been bombarded

by our Allies in their final advance towards Paschendale after Vimy ridge, it had rested unharmed further."

"But you can never count on what Fritz will do, or when he'll begin," remarked Blaine. Then as the girl went on, Erwin sat down suddenly as if something within him had all at once given way.

"Keep still, Mr. Erwin," she cautioned. "You're not well yet. As I was saying we got through the lines all right. If either my sister or the Baron had gone, they would have been made prisoners at least. I was a Red Cross nurse. We had done good work over there and even the Germans were well disposed. But if it wasn't for Brenda, I hardly know how we'd have managed Brenda is a—a whole team, you know." She pressed her servant's worn hand as she continued. "We reached the chateau, secured the papers with out much trouble, for Brenda, being an old family servitor, knew where to find them. That very night, while we were in these underground rooms, the Germans began dropping bombs all about.

"It appeared that the Allies from over our way had gotten to raiding behind the lines, not knowing we were here, of course. Otherwise they would not have begun, for the Baron is highly respected among the Belgians and other Allies Why not? He is one of their King Albert's main leaders. Well, after that we simply had a terrible time. First one side, then the other would either fight overhead, or pass to and fro, dropping bombs here and there. Oh, it was terrible!"

"Poor child!" This from Brenda. "She no harm no one; but dem Boche, he no care what he do or where he do it. Ally not know either."

"Well, we have been here ever since. Now you have come, perhaps we may somehow find a way to get out."

Here Stanley suddenly entered, looking strangely resolved. Above, the explosive noises had gradually died out. Looking at Blaine, he said:

"Lafe, I have fixed up that German's Fokker All it needs is more gasoline and there's still some in your tank and Orry's.

If you don't care, I'll fly that Fokker over our lines before morning and manage to bring some help. Neither of you are strong enough to go and I understand Fokkers pretty well. What say?"

"That won't do at all," exclaimed Erwin, making another violent effort not only to stand but to walk. All at once he tottered and would have fallen, but Brenda caught him, placing him back on the cot.

"That'll do for you, Orris," began Blaine. "Shucks! I feel quite pert. Just you watch me!"

But it turned out that Blaine was, if anything, weaker than his friend, and silence gave consent to his first proposal. Even Miss Daskam assented, adding: "I hope when you do return with help, sir, that it will be sufficient to enable Brenda and me to accompany you."

For the first time Stanley seemed to catch the wistfulness in her eyes and tone. He impulsively took her hand, saying:

"Believe me, Miss Aida—Daskam, I mean," (She had already whispered to him her full name), "if any of us gets back out of this mess, you may be sure you will be among them—"

"And Brenda, too?"

"Brenda, too! If I know anything of our folks back at the aerodrome, we will have plenty of help."

In another minute he was gone. Brenda went with him to help about the gasoline, and in an short time, under her pilotage, he reached an open spot where he could rise.

They heard the whirring of his wings; he was gone.

CHAPTER 14

Two Perilous Night Trips

It may be said that, once up in the air, Stanley lost no time in heading into the west-southwest. He knew the way, and though it was yet hardly midnight, he divined the safest way for him to make the familiar aerodrome was to get there as soon as possible, regardless of consequences. The night, though foggy, was sufficiently starlight to aid in his sense of direction. It was hardly likely that there would be further bombing raids that night, but one was never certain what the Boches might attempt. Witness their recent raid upon the old chateau, although they might know that planes had recently landed there.

After the North Sea Wind fog, a general calm had settled down upon that death-scarred region. Over the front and about No-Man's-Land an occasional flare or star-shell would go up. One of these came unusually close to the swiftly moving Fokker. Immediately after that came bombing from Archies stationed along the enemy front. Among these some, either accidentally or by design, sent bursting shrapnel all around him. He heard the wings being struck repeatedly but, knowing his great speed, he hoped to be out of range almost at once.

With the sound of big guns the whole front was lighted up here and there with flares and starshells, many being sent up from shell holes concealed from all but their own side.

More than that; for Stanley, leaning far over to scan the earth below, suddenly saw men rushing some kind of a gun up a steep incline. Where was that? It could not be the Appin-courte Bluff, for that was now in our hands. But he recalled another elevation near the small stream behind.

"Can it be the Boches have tunnelled to that former an-other advancing post?"

Further thought was interrupted by a brilliant flash and a dull report just underneath. At the same time he felt sharp stings pierce his arms now stretched outside the fuselage as he leaned over. Something like a needle seemed to pierce his brain. In the same instant he was aware that in his eagerness to reach the base quickly, he had permitted his plane to ap-proach the earth a great deal nearer than before.

He was tilting his rudder upward, while feeling at once that he was about all in. But feverishly he gripped wheel and controls, more with feet than hands, for he was growing more helpless each passing second. The flashings below had shat-tered into many small scintillations as they shot upward, while something sharp and metallic was rattling among his planes.

But he was mounting, he knew that. Dizzily, he managed mechanically to turn the plane towards where he knew the broad aerodrome was situated.

"Hope they haven't hit my tank," he maundered. "I—I'll get there—" But that was all he did say, for unconsciousness was coming fast.

At the same time he sensed somehow that the Fokker—al-ready well peppered by his own crowd on that same day—was listing, sagging, so that at last he could hardly keep his seat.

"I—I'm goin'—goin'," he kept reiterating in his mind. "Goin'—go'n—go—" He lapsed into complete unconscious-ness, with his last sentient movement pressing the wheel and controls downward and towards the left, where he finally half fell, as we have seen before.

Byers and the orderly bore him quickly to the near-by dormitory, where many of the fliers were temporarily lodged. Senator Walsen and the girls followed, while some of the me-chanics attended to the crippled Fokker.

In almost no time the surgeon on duty was there with two of the Red Cross nurses. Though unconscious, Stanley was restless, uneasy, evidently worrying. He muttered unintelligibly, tried to break forth more loudly, but for the present was unable to make any meaning clear to the others.

"What gets me," remarked Byers while watching the deft manipulations of the surgeon and the nurses, "is how he came here alone and in such a rig. Why, that Fokker must have been taken from Fritzy! Why didn't he return in one of our own machines? Where are the others? I tell you, Senator, there is trouble afoot; I feel it in my bones!"

As may be imagined, both Andra and Avella were much concerned, though neither would admit it to the other or, for that matter, to any one else. Only once Andra, clinging to her sister, whispered timidly:

"Sup—suppose this poor chap never does revive, Vella? How will we ever know?"

"We've got to know, Andra. Got to—that's all I can say!"

By these two whisperings aside each girl was conscious of betraying to the other some sign of that deep, sudden interest with which at least two of these dashing young aviators had inspired them. And they, the fair daughters of a United States Senator! Verily strange and surprising are the freaks of Cupid. But of this more later. The physician was still busy over the slowly reviving patient, when the watchful orderly hurried in to where the captain was watching and waiting.

"I thought I better go out and take a look, sir. While I was out at the observation there came some signal flares out of the nor'-nor'east. I wasn't certain, sir, so I waited. Along came another flash, adding our most private code signal. After that I dared not hesitate, nor had I time to run to you without answering. So I—so I—"

"So you answered, eh? Well, that's all right. Did you show a flare, also in code?"

"You bet, sir! I think it's one of our missing men that

may have lost his way. Better come out with me. He'll be landing next."

Without another word Byers accompanied the orderly out to a point near the observation post, and almost instantly they heard the whir of approaching wings, evidently spiralling down from greater heights.

"Give him a light lad." said Byers to the orderly. "He knows where we are, but in this black night he might hit some building or the fence.

Down on the gravel ran the assistant, followed by Byers, who saw the flare go up. In a minute a tattered triplane emerged into the light and made an easy landing not far from where the unconscious Stanley had previously been carried from his Fokker to the casual dormitory.

Almost before they reached it two of the night watch among the mechanics arrived and lifted out our old friend Buck Bangs from Idaho. He was unconscious, the cause being a body bullet wound on the right side, the bullet being later found bedded in the back of the seat in his Nieuport.

The machine was riddled even worse than Stanley's Fokker, but fortunately not in any vital parts, nor had the planes, though perforated like a sieve in many spots, been injured in any way to impair their vitality for the frames and joints were all right.

"Take him up to the Casual Dormitory boys," ordered Byers. "Careful! We don't know how badly he is hurt."

Up they bore him, leaving the machine where it stood. Into the dormitory he was carried and laid on a vacant bed near the now recovering Stanley. The latter had shown signs of resuscitation and now, as they bore in poor Buck, his head hanging helplessly, his limbs limp and unstrung, Stanley opened his eyes for the first time. They fell upon Buck, on whom the full light happened to shine brightly.

"Buck—there's Buck!" gasped the wounded observer. "Where'd he come from?"

At this instant Vella, happening to glance up, saw Buck's

pallid face as it rested on the arm of one of his supporters who was helping to place him on the ready cot. She gave a convulsive gasp, seized Andra by the arm and pushed forward, hardly sensible of where she was, but only that this youth from the State next to her own was apparently fatally stricken.

"Stay with me, Andra," she murmured. "I may faint. I don't want to say! Is he alive? Oh, Andra; does he live?"

Fully alive to the peculiar exigencies of the situation, and deeply sympathizing with Avella, Andra clung to and supported her sister until both were themselves again. Thereafter they watched, helped when they could, and as a rule kept as quiet as mice. It was really a ticklish situation for two young girls, both among the elite of official society in Washington, though transferred of their own volition to strange scenes and duties in this foreign land. Sisterly always, they now clung together more than usual.

"Is—is poor Buck dead?" asked Stanley, gaining strength with each word. "He left us to raid some more Boches and—and get help."

"The young man is all right." This from the surgeon who had just finished his examination. "He will pull through with good nursing. It's a bullet wound between the ribs and I f ear, although I'm not certain yet, that in passing it pierced the lungs. It has gone out at his back, near the shoulder, and that's a good thing. Leaves a clean Wound."

By degrees Buck was brought to, revived by a tonic, braced up by a subtle injection of some kind, after which his wound was carefully, thoroughly, and scientifically dressed.

Laying back after this, the first person on whom his sleepy eyes opened was Stanley, now raised on one elbow, so strong had he already grown, regarding Bangs much as one might look at some one supposed to be dead, but returned to life.

"Hello, Buck!" Stanley actually tried to sit up in bed. "When we saw you put out up in them clouds, I sure thought you were a goner!"

Buck weakly shook his bead, but was restrained by the

nurse from trying to talk. "No use!" he whispered wearily. Then his eyes sought that sweet girl again . She was still looking at him. He gave a sigh of satisfaction and almost immediately fell asleep.

All at once Stanley seemed to remember what he had come through a flying death for. He cursed his forgetfulness, then said aloud:

"I want to see Captain Byers. It—it's important. Please send for him."

But Byers, already alert, was stepping close and; saying:

"If it is important, go ahead. But if it can wait—"

"But—it can't wait, Captain," pleaded Stanley. "They sent me 'cause they couldn't come. All our planes were bombed from overhead. Had to use Fritzy's little old Fokker after we got him and his machine. Believe me, they're a tight place, and there's two women with 'em, one of them an American girl from Chicago; t'other a good old Belgian."

"Go ahead, my man," urged Byers.

Thereupon Stanley, refreshed by a mug of real Red Cross French wine, proceeded to relate a succinctly as he could all that the reader now knows Irwin, and Bangs, so far as Stanley had known. Also their varied adventures after following the defeated Hun down amid the ruins of the old baronial chateau.

"Believe me, sir, they are in bad shape," continued Stanley earnestly. "Both them chaps are clean knocked out for the time being, though I know they will be able to travel by the time we get back there."

"You say there are women there, too?"

"Yes, sir; two of 'em. One is sister to the wife of the Belgian baron who owns the whole chateau and estate. They got a permit somehow and came through the lines; but in view of recent troubles around there they don't know how to get back. "I'm sure sorry for them."

"What did they go there for, knowing the Germans controlled all that territory? Had they no better sense?"

"So far as I could understand, they went in the first place for some important papers hid away there, and which the Boches don't know of."

"Private papers or papers pertaining to the, war?"

"Don't know, sir. All I know is that they said, they had left safe and were to bring them back if they ever do got back."

Of course the surrounding group were listening. Among these was a runty, pockmarked, weasel-eyed little chap who went by the name of Pete, and whom was not much thought of, being considered by those who knew him best to be more than half German by blood. Be this as it may, he now began to edge outward from the group and gradually gravitated towards a side door.

However, he was already watched, and by no less a one than Byers' orderly. Ever since the escape of Hans, every one suspected of German connections had been under secret but thorough espionage. When Pete went out at one door the orderly emerged at the other in time to see Pete making for the observation post.

"What can the fool want there?" wonder the orderly. In less than a minute he was satisfied for, drawing from his pocket a peculiar flare Pete lighted and sent it up, where it shivered into different coloured flashes, doubtless some kind of cheap signal to warn his countrymen that some big was up. Perhaps also a signal for some one to meet Pete somewhere. But the orderly had even less patience than discretion. In two more minutes he had Pete under arrest and bound for the guard house. One of the mechanics aided the orderly and despite Pete's protests, he was shut up for the night.

When Byers was told of the matter he first stared, then frowned, and finally laughed, saying:

"I forgot that you had only been on duty here for a few days. When I am detained here late, I have Pete or some of the hands send up a certain kind of flare right down to where I live. That warns 'em I won't be back before breakfast. Now trot right back now and let Pete out, sending him to me. He knows this neighbourhood where Blaine and Erwin are now. We may need him -and need him bad."

Much crestfallen, the orderly obeyed, finding Pete fast asleep in a corner, nor much put out when he found what a mistake had been made.

When they reached the gravelly levels near the hangars, two of the largest biplanes in the aerodrome were already drawn up ready. In each of these planes an experienced pilot was in the act of taking his seat. One of these pilots was Byers himself.

"Come here, you, Pete!" called the captain, half laughing at Pete's perplexed face. "You in here with me—see?"

"You take me to Boche 'stead of black-hole? I no do harm anyone."

Pete spoke in a whining, ingratiating tone, but Byers only laughed, saying:

"You are right, Pete. A mistake was made." Then turning to Stanley, who had insisted on coming for final admonitions, "This is my friend Pete, once servant of Baron Savahl. That I know. He is small and light. He will guide us with the assistance that you, Stanley, have given me. Brodno also is particularly well acquainted with that part of the Belgian frontier. Get in, Pete!"

"But, Captain, how can we spare you?" This from Stanley anxiously.

"You will have to spare me. Sergeant Anson is handy, too. In the early morning, if you see signs of our return, it would be well to send out a few scouts. But we shall return. Those plans are too important to King Albert of Belgium and our Allies here to risk any more uncertainties than can be avoided."

"Are you sure of what you speak? I thought, from what those women said, that they were private papers."

"Private they may be, in a sense. But they are important enough to all of us, when you consider how vital they are to certain knowledge necessary for our leaders to have in regard to a further offensive which I believe is contemplated. Now back to bed, boy. You've warned us and we who are well will do all that is needful."

About this time Brodno, waiting impatiently, gave a signal and the plane, propelled along gravel by mechanics, soon rose lightly in the air. Byers, having hauled Pete in, followed suit, waving good-night to Senator Walsen and the ladies. In another minute both big biplanes were lost to sight, so swiftly did they vanish in a easterly course under the starlit heavens, shimmer of grey haze hugging the lower just above the earth.

CHAPTER 15

Making Ready for Another Forward Drive

After Stanley's sudden departure from the ruined chateau, the two boys fretted ineffectually. Stanley was an observer, not a real pilot; he might get into trouble; so worried first one and then the other.

"It seems to me, gentlemen," began Miss Daskam, "that instead of fretting over this you better remain quiet and thus regain your strength the sooner. We may need it yet."

"Allons, madame," began Brenda, speaking to the girl, yet carefully refraining from looking at either of the boys, "we cannot tell what time the Boches may break in on us. After that young man went up in the German plane, I am sure I heard the sound of far-away explosions. We are between the lines, yet off to one side, where the enemy are fond of raiding. It was so a year ago when some of us still made our home in or close to the chateau. We didn't mind the raiding. All they did was to rob us of what little stock we had left. But now, since they began the bombing that has finally ruined the Baron's home, nothing and no one is safe. Ah—what is that?"

But it was nothing much; yet it only typified the general nervousness of the situation. Distant firing along the course they figured that Stanley would take tended to make even the boys uncertain as to whether he would get home or not.

"Anyhow, we may as well make up our minds to have to stick it out here at least until tomorrow, or more likely tomorrow night. If they come they must come in force, or we will never be able to make a get-away." Thus spoke Erwin.

After more or less futile remonstrance, discussion and what not, they finally settled down for the remainder of the night, the boys insisting upon giving up the only habitable room to the women, though the latter urged that the young men take at least a blanket or so along. Blaine, being somewhat the stronger, declared that he would remain on watch for the first two hours, adjuring Erwin to get all the sleep he could.

"Another thing; we haven't got much grub along. I don't know how much the women have, but if it is scarce we must remember them."

In five minutes Orris was breathing heavily, taking full toll of slumber, for he was not so very strong and the day's happenings had exhausted him greatly. Blaine sought shelter under another angle of the basement, and after a vigorous struggle against somnolence, finally dropped off.

After that the old ruin was silent. Midnight passed. Unceasing silence reigned. Suddenly there came a sound of planes coming down from the upper air.

Finally a fretful voice rose up stridently, recklessly, saying through a muffled megaphone:

"Ho, there—below! Start up a flare—a light, anything, so we can know where and how to land."

Fortunately Erwin, who had really slept the longest, was roused by the closing words. He heard the sound of wings above, and at once apprehended. He had no flare, and no means at immediately to make a light. What should he do? Suddenly he remembered that Blaine carried a brilliant hand searchlight. In another instant he was rummaging about among Blaine's personal effects where he lay snoring.

"G'way—what you doin'? Who are ye, anyhow?"

While so ran the sleeper's drowsy remonstrances Erwin secured the searchlight, and an instant later was sending its white rays upward. A minute later the black shadow of a huge bi plane hovered in a circle over the wide expanse of what once had been a trim lawn, but was now a desert of dirt, ashes, and crumbling masonry loosened from the walls.

Meantime the added noise, further awakening Blaine, sent him scurrying to rekindle the dying fire they had made earlier in the night. By the time this was blazing one plane had alighted and the other was settling down further out. From these big planes stepped Captain Byers and Sergeant Brodno, both nervous, watchful, alert, and very wide awake.

To say the boys were pleased to see them would be to put it mildly. In a few words the state in which Stanley and Bangs had reached the Station was told, when Byers, evidently on edge by the peculiar situation wherein they were now involved, spoke up sharply.

"Where is that Chicago girl with her attendant? Also those papers? And how is it that I find you two so sleepy, way out here in the midst of the Boches? Don't you know we've had all sorts of trouble dodging in here so they wouldn't catch on? Oh—h! Who is that?"

Captain Byers whirled and found that he was confronting a smiling young girl, already bundled up as if for a journey. Behind her stood the substantial form of Brenda, also well wrapped against the night's chill and mist.

Confusedly Blaine presented the captain and Brodno, the latter grinning amusedly. In fact, this affair had been more of a lark to the American Pole than to Byers, who was oppressed with a sense of responsibility.

"We'll have to divide up, and at once," said the captain. "In fact, ever since Erwin used that searchlight to show me the way down, I haven't felt that we were safe here. Therefore I say all aboard just as soon as we can be loaded in—what is that?" as a sharp staccato of shocks rose from Brodno's machine, the result of his tinkering with his air-exhaust. Even as he made haste to stop them, time being all important, Byers was placing the two women in his own plane, saying:

"It will be crowded, but you can stand that for a time, I

guess. But—say! Hold on! I forgot. You have some important papers somewhere?"

"Yes. Brenda has them in her bosom. You may be sure we did not forget those. Are they all right, Brenda?"

But here Brenda jumped up in the observer's manhole, and began hastily fumbling among the folds of her ample garb. With a sudden half scream she sprang out, seized the searchlight from the astonished Erwin and made a dash for the basement again.

"Is what she is after important?" asked Erwin of Miss Daskam, who was fidgeting uneasily. The girl nodded, adding:

"It may be; I cannot tell. How careless! Among those papers are some very important plans that have reference, I think, to things our side wished to do later on. Oh, dear! Will we ever get away?"

"God knows—I hope so. It seems I hear sounds to the eastward. Ah—there they come again!"

Both Brenda and the captain, who had followed her, were returning. He was stuffing a paper which Brenda had surrendered after some persuasion into his breast pocket.

"All in!" called Byers. "No time to lose now."

Again the women re-entered the captain's machine, who at once started off along the level, open ground, at the same time calling on the men to use the searchlight so he might rise successfully. Up they went, and right after them came Brodno, with Blaine and Orris, now in the observer's seat, feeling more comfortable as be laid his hand on the Lewis gun ready to his use. Brodno had another. Both were listening to the sounds which Erwin had noticed when with Miss Aida. Byers passed them with a gentle rustling as of wings.

"Boys," he called back, "our defence rests mainly upon you. I have not only these women to see after but also papers—papers most important to our side in the next offensive. Of course I'll fight, if I have to. But the main thing is to get safely back and—"

His further words were lost on the wind as the captain raced ahead, bound as straight as possible for their own lines.

"We will keep right on his tail, boys," said Brodno. "That noise behind is Fritzy starting on a raid, no doubt. If he gets too close we must either keep him back or lead him off after us."

The noise of whirring propellers increased rapidly. Doubtless scouting planes were out. As a rule, they are faster than the big biplanes. In view of this, Byers presently began to mount higher, the rear plane maintaining its level with a view of attracting the notice of the pursuing Germans. Then came a spatter of machine gun bullets that rattled about their ears until Blaine, from his rear position, opened on the Boches in turn.

After that the pursuit of Byers ceased, for Blaine and Brodno, with their two weapons, aided by Erwin, who manipulated a Lee-Enfield rifle, kept the three scouts busy for a time. A plane is a shaky place from which to aim a rifle, but Orris, having had much practice at the training butts, soon laid out one lone pilot and his scout went trailing guideless out of range and action.

But about this time there came the heavier rumble of Archies from below, and presently shrapnel began tearing into the wings of the biplane.

"Up we go, boys!" said Brodno. "I guess Byers must be well on over by now."

But about this time they heard the sounds of gun spatter far up above, and mounting rapidly they saw two more Fokker scouts trailing after Byers, who not only mounted still higher, but put Pete at the aft machine gun, taking Miss Aida over inside his own manhole.

We haven't said much about Pete, for he was really timid, and lay low wherever he was placed, without a word. But when he came over where Brenda was and that sturdy Belgian watched his timid attempts to fire the machine gun, she was disgusted.

"Pete, you no good! Have you forgot how the Baron hated a coward? Let me in there!" She shoved Pete aside, took charge of the gun herself and presently Byers was gratified to hear its active rattle as Brenda rather clumsily yet effectually opened upon the Germans. Pete assisted, handing fresh sheaves of ammunition and otherwise making himself useful.

"Where you been, Pete?" she asked. "Why you leave us all?"

"I wanted to learn to fly. Americaines, they give me a chance."

The other plane, now spiralling upward, came within range of the Fokkers, and altogether the united firing from the two big biplanes was too much for the Boches, so they gradually retired with a loss of one plane, whose pilot Erwin had disposed of, as we have seen.

Half an hour later they quietly dropped down at the aerodrome. The first grey hues of morning were just diffusing a lighter pallor and the stars were already dimming when on the deserted levels in front of the hangars the biplanes finally came to rest. Then out from a sentry box came the captain's orderly, who seemed much astonished.

"Well, sir, I didn't look for you all back so soon. I rather feared that you might have to remain away another day."

"We had ladies to look after," remarked Byers. "That made us hurry back sooner. Here is Pete, of whom you thought such dreadful things. Pete is learning. Now, while we take Miss Daskam and her maid to their quarters, I want you to go to the through line to Dunkirk, and ask for Baron Suvahl. He should be somewhere about there, if we have been rightly informed."

After that the captain with characteristic courtesy took the two tired yet grateful women to the women's Red Cross station and left them in kindly, congenial company. It was here Senator Walsen and his daughters were staying. When they and Miss Aida became acquainted at breakfast next morning it was astonishing how many mutual acquaintances they discovered, yet mostly back in the dear old country across the ocean.

About the middle of the morning a tall, spare, resolute young man, accompanied by a plainly garbed lady, his wife, met Captain Byers at the latter's office. Simultaneously there came two other personages plainly garbed in Belgian costume, yet most distinguished aside from that.

There was a certain respect, almost deference, in the way Baron Suvahl and his wife met the King, for one of the visitors was really King Albert of Belgium. His wife, the queen, was even more democratic. In fact, in the manner of all, including the Americans, was that which marked them as fully tinctured with the true democratic spirit that this war has so fully brought out among all the Allies.

Several of the British and French generals dropped in. And there were sundry secret and semi-secret conferences, one result of which was the sending out that night of a number of our airmen on secret scouting trips, none of which, however, resulted in much aerial fighting but embraced a deal of sly spying upon enemy positions and also various "look-ins" behind the lines.

Among other things Erwin, Blaine, Bangs, Brodno and others were adjured by both Captain Byers and Sergeant Anson to be ready with their machines for real active service at any time.

On the second night came a quiet meeting between certain French, British, and American commanders. As the boys in the aerodrome sauntered about the grounds, noting the drawn shades in the windows of the headquarters office, and marking the lateness of the hour before the consultation closed, they felt that things were drawing to a head on that sector, and that they, the eyes of the army, would be expected to do their part and even more, if necessary.

Senator Walsen, instead of going back to the capital as he had intended, was drawn into the conference, while the ladies remained quiescent but more and more expectant, though of what they hardly knew. Perhaps the good young queen expressed the general sentiment among her sex, when she said to the small group gathered about her at the half shabby quarters where she and the king temporarily received their friends,

"We never know much as to what is about to go on, but we are always warned never to be unduly surprised at anything. Always make the best of everything—that is all we can do and what we must do.

CHAPTER 16

The Conflict

For another day many quiet yet suggestive movements were made in the vicinity of these headquarters where most of the activities of this tale have taken place. That night secret word went out among certain picked birdmen that they were to be ready that night for literally anything

"What do you think is up, anyhow?" asked Erwin, who had been busy with a mechanic nearly all that day putting his favourite scouting flier machine in complete readiness.

"How should I know?" snapped Anson, hurrying by. "We know we gotter be ready any old time, night or day. I 'opes I may niver see Blighty ag'in though, ef I don't think we're in fer somp'in' damn big and hard." And he passed on, vouchsafing Orris a wink that might mean anything.

That next night other planes from near-by sectors began flitting in here, there, until, with the planes already at the aerodrome, there must have been at least fifty of the various types of battle and scouting planes on hand. Many of the airmen were French, many British, not a few Americans, inclusive of the Lafayette Escadrille, composed mainly of men from overseas.

The early evening passed, the dark hours flitted by, and so came midnight with a long line of planes stretched far and wide over that war-scarred expanse. Here and there the pilots had gathered in little groups, receiving their last instructions from majors, captains, lieutenants, even sergeants of the various aviation corps or squads who had, in turn, received theirs from commands higher up.

Some of these groups were studying maps and photographs which had been made by recent reconnaissance trips and prepared for distribution among those whose task it was to proceed along the various lines thus indicated.

One group near the centre of the line deserves attention. There was Erwin, Blaine, Bangs, Brodno, all seemingly in fine fettle, gathered over sundry maps, photos, and instructions. Amid these was Captain Byers, somewhat at the rear, conferring with Senator Walsen, who had still deferred his return to Paris, more than likely through the persuasions of his daughters.

Where were they? Let us look more closely among the airmen. Who is that whispering coyly to Sergeant Bangs, who stands cap in hand, despite the frosty night air? He talks earnestly, rapidly, western fashion, ending with"

"I don't know bow I shall come out of all this! But I do know that Montana and Idaho are side by side. May I come to see you then?"

"Yes, provided that neither you nor Mr. Blaine forget that Paris leave which I feel sure you will get." And Avella Walsen blushed prettily. "But I must go back to father now. Goodbye." She was gone, flitting towards the rear not unlike a star gleam in Buck's eyes as she vanished, leaving him to sigh regretfully.

Near by Andra Walsen had taken an almost tearful leave of stalwart Ensign Blaine, now completely restored, and naturally keyed up by a prevision of the night's probable happenings.

Further to the right both Brodno and Erwin, still fussing round their respective planes, were interrupted by no less a personage than the Belgian Queen, accompanied by Baroness Suvahl and her sister, Miss Daskam, who had come round to them on their night round of visiting encouragement which they were making among their acquaintances that night.

"We are so glad to see you boys on duty again," said the

Queen, who was most unassuming and kindly in manner. "Both the King and the Baron had to leave again for our front, but I persuaded them to let us bid you lads good cheer and Godspeed in your risky night's adventure."

Meanwhile Miss Daskam was whispering to Erwin:

"Do you remember the last night at the chateau, how you would not take all the quilts I wanted you to, though the night was cold and we had plenty?"

"Indeed I do, miss!" Orris was grinning now. "I just knew we did not leave you and Brenda enough! Did we, Brenda?"

Turning to that stalwart guardian in petticoats who watched over the two sisters from Chicago, one of whom had married a Belgian nobleman, Brenda shrugged her massive shoulders.

"You must ask Mademoiselle Aida. I was mooch too warm; yes, vera mooch. Yes la—la! We Flemings know what cold is more than what it is to be too—too warm. Don' you bodder, sar!"

And so the many more or less friendly, even solicitous conversations went on until the midnight hour had fled. By then the groups of friends and visitors had melted back to the rear into the misty regions where lay the small French village that had sheltered them together with the aerodrome itself.

It might have been one o'clock or later when a bugle sounded. Up and down the long, long line aviators were scrambling into their machines while the sputter and throb of many engines punctured the night air. Some of these engines had as much as three hundred horse-power. The long continuing roar was nerve grating, yet inspiring. Swarms of small scouting machines were humming, spitting; these were the vipers or wasps of the air service.

The fleet commander and his observer had taken their places and soared into the night air. The other machines, some fifty odd in number, swiftly followed him into the misty heavens, all manoeuvring like a flock of swallows until the air formation was at last right. Then a crack from the commander's revolver, and they were off like bees, following the queen, straight for the far-off enemy lines.

Much ammunition had been distributed, for they were going on a general bombing and foraging expedition over those trenches upon which the now ready offensive was to be let loose. Dimly they rose up, up, still up, six thousand, eight, even ten thousand feet, the last height mainly for the fighting scouts, the battle and bombing machines keeping lower down.

Over No-Man's-Land they flew towards the battle-torn trenches behind which lay the Boches. Tiny specks began to rise up far to the eastward in the German rear. They were the enemy planes coming to meet them. In number they seemed to be somewhat equal to our own fleet. The Allies might have fought these, but such was not the present game. They were there to protect their side; while the Allies were out first to destroy, to smash the morale of the soldiers below, to shatter and mutilate and terrorize those in the trenches before our infantry, now probably starting out, should be where their own conclusive work would begin.

Those lads whom we have followed through these pages were flying close together, keeping well to the front, watching signals from the commander and ready, more than ready, each to do his part. With Blaine was Stanley, his observer, both closely watching. When over the first line trenches, they at once let go the first rack of bombs. All the other planes, in accord with their individual capacity, did the same. A veritable hell beneath was let loose by that swiftly moving line. Lower down came the signals and more racks of bombs were let loose. So swift were their movements that one might hardly see what results were being obtained; but from the yells, shrieks, explosions and clouds of debris below, it was evident that the destruction was great.

Lower and lower still they flew. Blaine's control was perfect. So was that of his subordinates. Bangs himself, excited yet steady as a clock, was talking to his plane as a cowboy might talk to his pony. Machine guns could now be used most effectively. The cleaned, burnished mechanism was already vomiting death. in showers upon the trenches below. Their spitting, purring roars were drowning out the whir of the engines.

All at once Blaine saw to his left a spurt of flame shoot upward from below, and almost simultaneously a blinding glare arose from Brodno's plane. For an instant he caught sight of the Polish face, ashen grey as the night above, under which the fight was going on. His petrol tank had been hit from an Archie below and exploded. Another burst of flame and his plane swooped dizzily towards the mangled earth below.

"God help him!" gasped Lafe. "That must be the end of poor Brodno!"

Down it went, zigzagging crazily. All at once it dropped like a plummet. For an instant Blaine felt sick; then he recovered. His own situation, and that of Stanley, Erwin, Bangs and the rest was not less risky. Yet only one thing was there to do. Fight it out—fight it out, to victory—or death.

Then all at once the German planes were upon them. Where and how they came was a matter of indifference. The thing was to meet and fight, to out-manoeuvre them if possible. In another minute they were dodging, diving, eluding, darting among each other, inextricably intermingled, yet now, on the whole, rising higher. Just over to the right of Blaine one of the Boche fliers was already dropping to the earth. Blaine saw and noted the cause. It was Erwin, rising from a dexterous side-loop to higher elevation, yet peering over at his fallen foe.

"Good boy," murmured the ensign. "He'll do! No use to worry about flying position now. It's fight or die!"

What the Allies mainly cared about now was to dodge the enemy fliers, and still pour the remainder of their explosives down upon the mangled trenches until the Allied infantry should come up. By this time Stanley, back at his old post, was whirling round on his seat for more racks of bombs. He had already used his own machine gun with deadly effect.

Blaine was reaching for another drum of ammunition for his Lewis when he saw Stanley lurch forward. He was hit. Not a word though; not even a struggle.

"My Gawd, man!" called Blaine. "Are you hit bad? Slip down under cover!"

No reply as the observer slowly sagged back and down into the manhole.

Then a sudden rage filled the stalwart American. He loved Stanley, who he knew was game to the core. Just then a German machine sped by full tilt, sending spatters of bullets right and left. Instantly Blaine tried the tail-dip, always risky yet worth while if successful. Doubling under the tail of the passing Boches—there were two of' them in the machine—Blaine came up right under the German's propeller, his own gun in straight line for the centre of the other's fuselage. As he came up he began a spatter of bullets that fairly riddled the body of the big Taube, and directly thereafter came a burst of flame so bright and searching that Blaine had to dip again, sidewise to avoid its scorching significance. The German's tank was exploding and in a mass of flames the two men fell, the skeleton of their machine about them as the whole dropped to the earth.

Hardly had Blaine cleared this aerial ruin than came the commander's signal to retire. Somehow, after that, Lafe felt that in a measure he had a certain revenge from the Boches for poor Stanley's death; for Stanley was dead—no doubt of that. At least so Blaine thought.

Up he mounted and presently saw Buck Bangs engaged with a rather clumsy German, who seemed bent upon peppering Bangs and his machine full of holes. He flew to Buck's assistance, when the German straightened out and made for his own rear, with Bangs in full pursuit. In his present mood, instead of returning with the rest of the home squadron, Blaine took after the German, and for five minutes there was a mid-heaven race towards Belgium. But Bangs, in his small scout, was easily the fastest and soon he and the German were engaged in a running duel.

All at once Buck signalled to Blaine in code:

"Leave this Boche to me. There's a train off eastward. See if you can't do something. Get up higher: you'll see better."

Mutely Blaine obeyed and, as he rose up another thousand feet, he saw more than one row of cars, upon a single track hurrying towards the front, whence already the distant bellow of earthly struggles was going on. Evidently the big Allied offensive was on. If he, Blaine, could hinder the troop trains from reaching the front trenches, it might be a big help to the infantry, that was now attempting its part of the big stunt.

Straightway the biplane, with the body of Stanley still nestling in the bottom of the observer's, manhole, was shooting downward in a gradual slant towards the two trains. One of these was filled with soldiers, at least a brigade, for the train was a long one. The one ahead seemed to be loaded with munitions and with artillery on the rear cars.

Swooping down closer, Blaine laid his plan. When within three hundred feet he saw some Archies posted at a crossroads who at once began firing. In his present mood he would have cared little for any obstacle as yet untried.

Above the noise of his propellers he detected something behind, and, turning, what was his amazement to see Stanley's ashen grey face peering up over the observer's seat. Blaine was startled, as if he looked at a ghost.

"Get down, boy!" he adjured. "You ain't strong enough. Get down! I've got a stiff job just ahead. Give me time and room."

Whether Stanley understood or not Blaine was not certain. But just then the stricken man crumpled back again into his former nest at the bottom of the manhole. A slow groan came up.

"Poor chap! He's in misery, no doubt. But I've just got to try this job—"

Just then the Archies began to cut loose, but Blaine went to zigzagging, at the same time increasing his speed, swooping still lower—lower. At last directly over the front train, with machine guns, Archies, and rifles peppering away at him, he let go with one side of his bomb rack. With the sound of the resultant explosion he wheeled and let go the other.

Both racks landed directly upon the leading train loaded, as Blaine suspected, with all sorts of ammunition.

Instantly he pressed the upward controls and his machine darted on towards the rear just in time to escape the tremendous blaze and roar as that string of loaded cars began to explode one after another. The noise, flames and confusion were indescribable. Regardless of the still up flying shrapnel and shot, the daring man turned loose the controls and instantly whipped into place another rack or two of bombs.

By this time he was directly in the path and, right over the long troop train already slowing down to avoid collision with the exploding ammunition train. This in itself was almost impossible, so closely had one train followed the other, a most incautious thing to do.

He felt that his big spread of wings offered too great a bombarding surface to the forces at the crossroads below, but he was bound to finish the job so well begun, no matter what resulted to himself and Stanley.

Still further down he went, and at the pivotal instant began again with the first rack of bombs. Down they flow, crashing upon car after car. Though half conscious of something at his rear and left, he did not dream the cause until, turning, he saw Stanley's pallid face contracting with pain. The observer was shoving forward the second rack into the essential groove for firing. Blaine in his baste had missed fixing it in the notch necessary for accurate discharge. At untold bodily cost to himself Stanley had again risen and completed the task, just in time for the second rack to fall along the rear half of the train, the last bombs crashing into the rear engine pushing the heavy train from behind.

So far as could be seen from above the wrecking of the two trains was complete. Amid the din of exploding munitions rose the cries of hundreds of wounded, dying men, while the debris of the burning wreckage was strewn up and down the single track for a mile or more.

As Stanley sank back again, more deathlike than ever, Blaine put on all his power and strove to rise. Still roared the anti-aircraft guns, the machine guns and the rest of the snipers below; that is, all that were still on the job after the terrifying disaster so deftly accomplished by Blaine.

The biplane would not rise to any great degree. But it would travel at a gentle upward trend and as rapidly as ever.

Off he flew, more than anxious to get out of; range from the vengeful fire that pursued him.

Another groan from Stanley. Blaine, looking back, saw the lad crumpling up with a new red stain trickling down his scalp.

"How I would like to help him!" thought the pilot. "But the only chance for either of us is to keep on and get out of this hell."

For a wonder there did not appear any more Boche fliers, and as soon as he was outside the immediate range of the Archies, Blaine found that he was sailing north-eastward over an opaquely indistinct expanse of country which he felt in his bones must be that of the foe.

CHAPTER 17

Buck and the Boche Aloft

Meanwhile what had become of Buck Bangs, whom we left following the Boche flier that had first assaulted him, but who soon seemed to have enough of the game?

The truth was that Buck, who was plucky to the core, did not want to give up and return to the home base any more than did Blaine. Both were fighters and loath to abandon what looked like success as long as there seemed a chance to win out.

As he had told the Walsen girl once, when she remonstrated with him upon his temerity in the face of what more than once looked like certain death:

"Reckon I don't know that, miss? You bet I do! But, somehow, death don't come just then and—and I keep on riskin' some more. I—I guess I'm jest built that way."

The German, who was rather clumsy, kept on along his eastward flight, with Buck in hot pursuit. Getting closer, Bangs again opened up with his Lewis. What was his surprise to see the clumsy German crumple up in his seat and fall forward, his hands and part of his arms out of sight, as well as the other could see in the starlit night.

"I believe I got him at last," thought Buck, manoeuvring to a closer position. "I'll fill him and his tank full of holes, then see what has happened."

But just before Buck came into position, the German's plane suddenly veered athwart the nose of the other and deftly dove almost directly downward. The turn was a surprise. But Buck instantly knew that no machine, unless some one was handling the controls, would do a thing like that. Instantly he knew that the clumsiness of that Boche must have been assumed for the purpose of inducing Bangs to follow, thus leading the two planes away from the Allied squadron.

"Fritzy is sharper than I gave him credit for being," thought Buck. "But he'll not get under me in that way without doing more stunts yet." Instantly the nimble scout machine darted upward, at the same time turning on its tail in such a way as to bring both opponents side by side with Buck now still higher up. By the time the German had gotten into a firing position Buck had his Nieuport slanted nose downward and pointing straight at the enemy. But scarcely had this been done, before the German was veering off to the left and sliding down, down with scarcely conceivable rapidity.

Instantly Buck was after him, and for several minutes the two spiralled, twisted, dove, looped and performed other aerial feats accomplished only by expert fliers. By this time both were undeceived as to the skill of their opponents. Each knew that his adversary was worthy of all the dexterity and strategy the other might employ.

And all this in the dark, as it were. That is, in the dark as darkness is in the upper air, a sort of transparent twilight, when the mists are either absent or the light haze is as a gauze curtain stretched between our eyes and an upper light beyond.

At length the German, no longer clumsy, but most expert, seemed to be waving something that looked white. Then came a low megaphone call that made Bangs wonder if his ears were all right. It came in good United States English.

"Hullo, you!" it began. "Let's rest a bit and have a pow-wow!"

Buck could still hardly believe that he really heard, and he hesitated. Finally he returned:

"Don't know you! You talk like us, but you act like a Hun. Can't trust you Huns further than you'd—"

"Aw-come on down! I'm tired of fightin' a will-o'-the-wisp like you. Been in Akron lately?"

"Don't know the burg. Montana's my stampin' ground—when I'm home."

"I used to live in Akron—worked in the rubber factories. Come on down. I know a good place. We can yarn there—mebbe have a *zwie-bier*."

The two machines were now hardly fifty yards apart, with the German rather lower down than Buck.

"Not much, old man! I don't know you, I say. Now—you watch out! I'm—"

But Buck never finished that sentence. The German, having consumed as much time as he thought proper with his hyperbolical peace propaganda, suddenly dove sideways, executing what is now known as the Emmelin turn, that would bring him, nose up, somewhat below and on the other side of Bangs.

But Buck was not to be caught napping by any Hun making seemingly friendly proposals. Before the German had more than half executed the manoeuvre, Bangs was already shooting upwards in a zigzag course and by the time the other had gotten into position, Buck was swinging round far above, from whence, to outdo the other, he pointed his Nieuport downward point-blank at the fuselage of the German's Taube.

Swiftly he came, apparently reckless of consequences. It so turned out that the Boche did exactly what Bangs thought he would do: tried to avoid the descending avalanche. His machine swung to the right, yet not enough to clear the other. Full tilt the Nieuport struck the nearly motionless Taube near the centre of the fuselage. Nieuports are strong and sharp in their prow, and the metal edge clove through the side of the German machine not unlike one destroyer ramming another.

At the same instant Bangs, pointing his Lewis gun obliquely downward, sent a spatter of bullets full into his opponent just before the collision occurred.

Smash went in the side of the Taube. An instant before, the

shower of bullets had penetrated not only the petrol tank but also the body of the too plausible German. Anticipating what might happen, Buck clapped down upon his rudder, reversing his engine, and drew back from the shattered enemy just in time to escape the burst of flame that almost at once enveloped both man and machine.

"I settled him, " panted Buck, almost breathless despite himself. "He may have lived in the U. S., but he lacked much of American love for fair play. I wouldn't have run into him if he had acted at all white."

So ran Buck's thought as he sat breathing heavily, watching the plummet flight of the dead German and his flame-shrivelling plane to the earth.

Rising again to a higher altitude, he surveyed the surroundings as well as the night's dim light would permit. Nothing to be seen anywhere. All at once Bangs thought of Blaine. Faintly he had heard the sound of explosions down near the earth; but whether the same were bombs, or guns, or if any other cause were responsible the lad did not know.

"Ought I to look him up or not?" he more than once asked himself. "No better chap anywhere than Blaine, or for that matter Stanley either."

Circling round a wide aerial expanse while cogitating along these lines, he thought he heard the sound of far-off explosions somewhere below. His timepiece showed that the hour was near three A.M. Daylight would soon be showing. In the far west and southwest the thunderous roll of artillery was incessant, mingled with sharper minor concussion of small arms, machine guns and musketry.

"That drive must now be in full swing," he thought. "Ought I to circle round there and see if I can do any good? Might take a squint at the Boche front and let our artillery know."

He was about to follow out this when another rattle from below came up. Somehow he felt that it might be connected with Blaine and Stanley, nor would the notion rest until he began to descend.

The course followed took him somewhat to the north of where the great battle was raging in the southwest, and presently he saw quite an expanse of war-torn forest underneath, or so it seemed from the height at which be flew.

Then a third explosion shattered the air, seeming to rise from directly below. Bangs hesitated no longer. Ascertaining that his petrol was still plentiful, he began gliding downward, over a hamlet or two, mostly in ruins, then over a few small fields, and at last over the scraggy trees. Suddenly he saw to the right a broad oval with what looked like a battered wall around it. It might have been three to four hundred yards in length, by half that in width.

The dim view perplexed him greatly as he flew, not more than from one to two hundred yards above this singular ruin, completely surrounded, as it seemed by forest, or the remains of forest.

All at once, gliding from out some deep shadows, something came rushing along inside this oval, and stopped. A moment later it appeared to rush again over the same course but in the opposite direction. All this dimly came to Buck, swinging easily along overhead. Then it was all clear to him at once.

"I'm certainly gettin' nutty," he owned to himself. "That's a plane. Looks like a biplane and it's trying to rise. Why in Hades don't it rise? Probably because it can't."

He knew that the Boche in his Taube had gone down considerably to the north-eastward. And the Taube was on fire. No doubt about that. This was not a hostile machine, was it? Bangs did not feel that it was. He had heard along that front tales of a big concrete oval, once erected in the small Duchy of Luxemburg, close to the town of Arion, which town was near a large area of forest. It had been constructed about the era when a revival of old-time Olympic games had roused more or less interest in a modern worldwide participation in the same, as a sort of antique revival of ancient times. Several celebrations had come off, notably at Athens, at Paris, and elsewhere. Then the interest died out but this concrete oval had remained.

After certain minor uses it had fallen into neglect. When war came that region became more or less ravaged, though somewhat off the track of the main struggles. And here was Buck hovering over this modern relic of an old-time futility, while below him was a mysterious plane trying to rise but apparently not succeeding.

With this train of thought, Bangs got out his remaining signal flares and flashed one of the code signals most in use among the Allied aviators along this front. His pulses leaped when it was answered. Before Buck could do anything more, there came the sounds of a much nearer explosion somewhat off to the south, fairly jarring the earth with its impact.

The plane below was now motionless. All at once a series of flashes came upward that Buck instantly understood as saying:

"You must be of our side. If not, I'll have to take a chance. We are out of petrol: tank 'prang a leak. Can you help us out?"

"You bet!" flashed back Bangs. "Got enough so that we can both get home again. Who are you?"

This last query was instantly replied to from below by the private sign denoting that the parties below were of such and such squad or escadrille quartered at Aerodrome No. —.

Buck drew a long breath, then he flashed forth his own number and began to descend. Nothing more happened until Buck brought his nimble Nieuport to a smooth standstill a few yards distant from a big biplane that Bangs at once recognized as Blaine's.

"Well, well!" he exclaimed, dismounting and hurrying across the intervening space. "Isn't this luck—why—why what's the matter, Lafe? Sick?"

But Blaine was only sick at heart. Already be had taken Stanley out of the observer's manhole, had laid the lad down, pillowing his head on a blanket, and was bending low, massaging Stanley's immobile limbs. Stanley's face looked deathlike under the flare of Blaine's flashlight.

In an instant Buck understood. Stanley had been wound-ed, perhaps mortally, during the course of the night raid. Blaine, being unable to keep on his course longer owing to the gradual draining of petrol from the tank as the en-gines consumed the heat, had managed to descend to this retired place.

With not more than a word or two of explanation, Buck also set to, and both lads did their best to revive Stanley, who had fallen again into unconsciousness. The deadly swoon had been strengthened by Stanley's effort to put the last rack of bombs fully in place during the train bombardment, as we have already seen.

They tried cold water, brandy, and also some medicine Buck produced from his own kitbag, but all to no apparent avail. Meantime the explosions to the southward were in-creasing and, worse still, were drawing nearer, though slowly.

"We got to get out of this," said Lafe at last. "While I put Stanley back in the biplane yon draw as much of your petrol from your tank as you can spare and put it in to mine."

"All righty oh! We got to get a move on, too. Look yon-der!"

A bluish-green roll of flame was moving along the plain beyond the forest, showing dimly above it certain flying specks that were undoubtedly airplanes, but whether hostile or friendly was not apparent.

"Course it's Fritzy, Lafe," was Bangs' comment who, after aiding Blaine to stow the wounded man as comfortably as possible in his own manhole, was already at work replenish-ing the biplane's tank from his own. "To be square, I'll divide up, giving you a leetle the most. We gotter to get back—eh?"

"If possible, yes. I don't hanker after a German prison camp. It would sure kill Stanley, if he isn't dead already."

By the time they had their brief preparations completed, the fire, steadily approaching, struck the edge of an open-ing through the woods and suddenly burst into tremendous flame, with an accompanying report.

"Wait, Lafe," cautioned Buck, for both were in their seats. "Let, me rise first. I'll mosey towards that fire. As for you and Stan—you make your get-away. Sooner you get back to the home plate, the more you'll be apt to do for Stan. Stan's a bully chap—durn 'im."

Up into the air rose the Nieuport, while Buck was thus delivering himself. Over towards the line of fires and the shadowy circling of planes he went while Blaine himself made an attempt to rise. What was the latter's consternation to find that his plane would not rise sufficient to clear the concrete oval by which the open space was surrounded!

"What will I do now?" Blaine almost gasped. "Must be something wrong with the machinery that I failed to notice."

Another explosion, much nearer, that seemed to tear up trees within the forest. At the same time he distinctly saw Buck's machine circling round and round, high up in the air, and directly over where the last explosion had occurred. It looked puzzling. But Lafe had no time just then to observe Buck's doings except that, during the last flash, the concrete oval had given way.

Meantime the biplane was trying to lift itself a trifle higher, and happened to be beaded towards where the explosions were occurring.

"Damn if he ain't droppin' bombs, too," Blaine gasped, then quickly solved the riddle of Buck's manoeuvres.

Without waiting further, but applying all his power, Blaine drove the biplane forward at full speed, at the same time using both forward and rear steering blades to assist further elevation of the prow.

"Will we make it," he asked himself. "If we do, what will we do then?"

Too late to consider pros and cons now. The die was cast, either for good or ill. Then, all at once, he saw Buck's small triplane rise at a marvellous speed, while from the south came several other planes, almost skimming the ground in their onward rush. Also, still further on, was a confused mass that was struggling rearward, though what it could be was puzzling. It was still too dark to distinguish things clearly when unaided by the fires.

A whistling, whirring swish swept startlingly near his own plane, now at last rising high over the ruins of the oval, forty yards of which were scattered over the earth. From this sounded a well-known voice through a megaphone:

"Follow me—you—Lafe! Boches ahead. Follow me—dodge 'em."

That was all, but it was enough.

CHAPTER 18

Back Home

Blaine knew good advice when it came. His own more cumbersome machine having at last the right slope for rising, even in its crippled state, did rise, and rapidly, so that Lafe was much encouraged.

Bangs, still overhead, darted forward at a startling pace directly for the nearest enemy plane that intuitively dodged. He swooped to the left and engaged in the subtle, lightning-like manoeuvres which so often accompany the opposing efforts of two skilled antagonists seeking to gain the advantage one over the other.

This, as it was intended, gave Blaine his first chance to rise uninterruptedly and gain such height and distance as he desired. Meantime the grey dawn was slowly growing, enabling him to see in the south certain masses of men, disordered, yet moving with a common impulse towards the east. Undoubtedly they were the retreating Germans, at last giving way before the offensive that had been launched upon them by the Allies early the evening before.

The series of explosions and flames that they had seen dimly, from the forest surrounded oval, was the destruction made by the enemy along the lines of their night's retreat. They were going back to what has become known as the famed Hindenburg line or base, which for some time marked the end of the now retirement of the Boche forces on the west front.

Having attained sufficient height, Blaine turned more westward; on account of Stanley, he was determined to make the shortest cut towards the home aerodrome. But here, too, another flock of enemy fliers was hanging over the advancing Allies so that Blaine, for sake of caution, rose up, up, still higher in the effort to avoid these new antagonists.

Looking back, Blaine now saw Bangs engaged, in fierce conflict with two of the rearward squad of Boche fliers. Again he admired the marvellous speed and dexterity of his chum as the circlings of the three were faintly apparent.

All at once came a burst of flame from one of the three and down went the burning plane like so many had gone before.

"Was that Buck," gasped Blaine, greatly excited. "The other two seem strangely harmonious. I must see more."

Round he wheeled and sailed towards the two remaining planes that were zigzagging about each other a mile or more in the rear.

At a speed of two miles a minute, Blaine found himself almost immediately being circled by the first plane, which was so much like Buck's that he at first distinguished no difference. What first aroused him was a roar of sound and a spatter of bullets that stabbed his planes as the stranger flew by.

"By hoky! It's a Boche!" Blaine was already manoeuvring to get some shots himself when from the second plane, came a code signal that instantly informed him of his first mistake.

"Go home!" the flashes commanded. "Leave, me to take care of Fritz."

Quick as a wink Blaine turned to the homeward flight again. But his plane moved heavily. Back again came the German, but Bangs suddenly intruded and the two scouts were soon banging, diving, dodging each other while Blaine, pursued his former course as best he might.

But his speed was strangely slow. He had trouble in maintaining an even flight, and there were more planes coming from the west. This was the rear squadron of Germans, that had been overhanging the Allied advance and signalling their own men further east.

"Buck and I—we'll be overwhelmed," thoughT Lafe. "I'm growing weaker. What the hell is the matter with me anyhow," meaning his planes of course.

But before the approaching Boches could surround Blaine or Bangs, still fighting his foe, there rose suddenly out of a cloud to the southwest a new flock of airplanes that instantly attacked the retreating foe.

All this time a terrific artillery fire was roaring out of the east, as the result of the Boches signalling from their rear squadron, now being rapidly whipped into flight by the new onslaught of Allied planes.

Where was Bangs? Just then Blaine saw the solitary Boche flier that had first attacked him and afterwards got it hot from Buck, speeding at a crippled pace towards the east. It passed Blaine who, having a sheaf of ammunition ready, turned loose upon it forthwith as it passed.

This was all it needed, for the foe, one wing swinging loosely, sagged earthward at a great pace, its pilot working frantically to keep on an even keel.

Two passing Allied planes each gave it a shower of bullets that caused it to topple over in mid-air, and go crashing down towards that grim and gory field below. But where was Bangs?

Blaine's anxieties were deflected from Buck to his own plane which at last turned earthward, not, crippled more by enemy aid, but—but—

"Why—confound it! I'm out of gasoline again. Well, here goes!" And he proceeded to carefully spiral down as gently as he could, no easy job when all motive power is suddenly exhausted.

He landed in a broad shell-hole and at once began to apply restoratives to Stanley who, very weak yet undaunted, asked where they were.

"Why, we're somewhere behind the Allied drive in what

was No-Man's-Land. But don't you bother! What I've got to do is to get you back to our base somehow."

"You've been mighty good, Lafe. I'll do my best to help by laying still and trying to get a mite stronger."

Here a groan was heard that caused Blaine to begin to investigate their immediate surroundings. Nearby was a wrecked plane in which we two Germans, one dead through the fall, and the other evidently dying. The dying man was conscious and had heard Blaine and Stanley talking together. Then came the groan. Instantly Blaine, rushing over, recognized him.

"Why, it is Herman Bauer!" he exclaimed, as much for Stanley's benefit as to show Bauer that he recognized him. "Anything I can do for you, Bauer?"

"*N-nein*—no," Bauer corrected himself. "I've got mine. *Himmel!* Eet vas to me coming I guess—vat?"

Here Bauer was seized by another convulsion that left him speechless, staring and all but dead.

Blaine surveyed him coldly.

"I didn't know you were much of a flier," he said. "Were you that chap's observer? Well, you must have photos, plans or something."

Then Blaine coolly proceeded to search both men, the dead pilot and the one about to die. Bauer's eyes gleamed with hate as he managed to say:

"*Gott strafe Englander!*" He choked, panting, then whispered with his last breath: "*Gott strafe Amerikanner—schwein—sch—*"

The whisper died away in a choking deep in the throat. Bauer was dead. He had paid the last great penalty. Blaine, still cool and unruffled, continued his search until he was in possession of all the two men had that was worth the trouble of taking. Among these were maps, air-craft photos of the Allied trenches and one valuable map the communicating transport and railway lines behind the new Hindenburg front to which Germans generally were retiring.

With Bauer dead and Stanley more comfortable, Blaine

began looking over his machine. It seemed all right but for lack of petrol and wings being more punctured and ragged than usual.

"Where can I get petrol?" he more than once asked himself. "I could either get on myself and join our men, or get back to the station. But I can't leave Stanley. Hang it all! What'll I do?"

Lafe was about to give it up for the present, when Stanley from his recumbent position said:

"Why don't you try that Boche plane? Seems like I heard Bauer say something about petrol. Then he swore because he could not get up. I didn't know then it was Bauer."

"Right you are, Stan! Why didn't I think of that before? I hope the fall didn't smash their tank."

It so happened the tank was nearly all right, only a little of the oil having leaked out through a twisted nut. Blaine got busy and in ten minutes he had transferred the German petrol to his own tank, and thereupon felt, as be phrased it, quite "like a new man."

Meantime stray shells were falling here and there, but none within a dangerous margin. Still, it would be better to get somewhere else.

"Come on, Stan," said Blaine. "I don't like these stray duds and coal-boxes. One of them might drop too near. Let me put you back in your manhole."

Before this could be accomplished, Blaine heard another nearing noise, at first high up in the air. Looking up he saw a tiny burst of flame from a dark, swirling object that was plainly descending fast, then faster still.

"Why, that must be a falling plane!" he exclaimed. "It's coming down mighty close, too. What'd I better do?"

Apparently there was not much to do for half a minute but to watch. And watch both he and Stanley did, wondering if it was enemy or friend, for the burning plane was careening, fluttering—not unlike a broken-winged bird. In the grey dawn they could see the pilot, still seated, dexterously manipulating every agency that might enable him to keep his balance without falling out.

Down, down he came, finally plumping to earth, just outside the broad shell-hole with a gentle crash. With this the flames burst up anew, enveloping the crushed wings, and rendering the very nearness a danger. But the goggled, leather-coated masked man had already sprung out, his personal belongings in hand, and stumbled up the outer slope of the crater. Suddenly he was halted by the stern command:

"Hands up—you!" There was no mistaking Blaine's voice by one who had often heard it before.

"Why, hullo, Lafe!" And Blaine and Stanley both recognized the wrecked intruder. "I thought you had made the home base."

Sure enough it was Buck Bangs himself, breathless from exertion, yet full of vim and energy still. He climbed nimbly up the slope and gripped Blaine's hand, then stooping, greeted the still weak, yet slowly recovering Stanley.

"I would have got there," said Blaine, replying to Buck's first remark, "but my petrol all at once gave out. I barely managed to save a fall by alighting here. How came you in this fix?"

"That's soon said. While I was fighting that plane that was after you and you were on the way home, as I thought, along came two other Boches. Well, we had it hot for a minute or so. I downed one somewhere along here."

"Yonder it lies," and Blaine pointed at the ruins of the other plane, near which lay Bauer and the other dead German. "Bet you'd never guess who one of them two Huns is." Lafe eyed Bangs quizzically.

"Nix! I ain't much on blind guessing. I saw my chap was crippled and I went back after the other, to keep him off you. I'd lost sight of you, but I reasoned you'd be on the way home. I knew you couldn't go very fast. Then all at once I saw I was afire. One of my wings had caught from something—probably an explosive shell. Well, I had to turn back. Meantime those planes arriving from our side had swept the

Boches clean off. I saw I wasn't getting much of anywhere and I just managed to light down here."

"But what about that chap over there?"

"Bother! I don't know beans about him; only if I helped bring him down I guess it was a good job."

"Better job than you think! You remember Bauer, the chap that was caught in the spy act back in the old station?"

Bangs nodded.

"He's one of the two over there," pointing at the airplane wreck, "and he was alive when I heard him. I went to him, but he was practically gone. Will say this for him though, he was a Hun all right, and he died cussing us all, Johnny Bull, Uncle Sam, as '*schwein, schwein!*' Oh yes, be was true German to the backbone. Between you and me I'm right glad that it fell to us to do him up, and that we will all know he got the reward due his abominable treachery." And Blaine nodded his head emphatically.

Bangs walked across, eyed the dead Hun a moment, and came back, saying:

"Will your plane carry us—but pshaw! You're out of gasoline, man!"

"No—we're not. Got a tank half full!"

"Too thin, old man! Why, then did you stop here? You didn't know I was going to drop down, and you knew Stanley ought to be in the hospital instead of lying here listening to you and me gabbing this way."

"Why haven't you got some invention, Buck?" Blaine was grinning as he rose up to prepare for early departure. "I 'lowed that if Bauer had enough gasoline to get this far, if his tank wasn't busted, he might have more. I took what they had and was about to leave when down you came. Come on—let's go!"

With great care Stanley was placed as comfortably as possible inside the biplane, which the two aviators trundled to the edge of the shell-hole. A moment later, with Bangs giving the plane a downward push, then leaping lightly up behind Blaine, they easily rose to a requisite height and glided over the shell-torn plain.

Far away to the east and southeast rumbled the roar of battle, while with the grey dawn, now mantling into rose pink, then red, and finally melting into the brightest of gold, at last came the morning's sun, leaping from its nightly nest and flooding half the world with the day's celestial glory.

Luckily their plane was not hit or in danger from the occasional shells that still came screaming over the lines across the scraggy war-torn land over which they flew. Stanley, though very weak, was still alive. Loss of blood was the main cause of his weakness. Upon recovering from his first state of coma, after sustaining his injury, he had borne the long, wearisome ride, the spatter and peril of conflict without complaint.

At Appincourte Bluff, where was now a base hospital, he was taken from the plane and put under adequate medical care. For twenty-four hours he dozed and slowly strengthened; but when be finally waked again to life and its daily events, there was Miss Daskam's fair young face at his bedside. Needless to state that Stanley's recovery was rapid under these auspices.

Meantime Blaine and Bangs made their further, way in the plane over the few miles intervening between the hospital and the aerodrome.

Most of the boys were away, scattered along the now advancing front but by night some of them began to straggle back. Poor Finzer and Brodno would never come back. That both Lafe and his companion well knew. But they had died like true men, fighting for the cause they believed in.

Captain Byers was also at the front, now many miles to the east. But the veteran Sergeant Anson was on hand and in partial charge. He it was who brought to the boys some sealed envelopes, saying:

"You chaps have been gone a goodish while. And you've managed to lose one bully scouting plane. But I guess you've done your bit all right."

"Well, sergeant," remarked Blaine quizzically, "I don't know what you'd call doing our bit. Buck here has brought down, with my help at times, several Boche planes. I managed to knock spots out of a troop and ammunition train or rather two of them. Better than all, we helped bring down another plane with two Huns in it, one dead, another dying. Guess who the last one was?"

Anson grinned, frowned, then shook his head.

"Bother the guessin'! I ain't as bally good at that as you Yanks. Was it any one we knows?"

"You remember Bauer?"

"That rotter what was found guilty of spyin' for the enemy? Yes, I knew the blighter, the traitor?"

"Well, he's dead. When his plane fell on fire, I had to drop down in a shell-hole back yonder. Bauer and his pilot had fallen near there just before. He was cussing us all out, Boche fashion. But it was from their machine that I got enough petrol to fetch us three safely back. So you see Bauer was some good after all. Of course he was a traitor and should have been hung."

"Well, you two haven't done so bad. Before Senator Walsen and his daughters left they gave me these things for you two, if you had the luck to get back. And Captain Byers, before going on this raid, left this permit, together with all necessary papers for you two to go on leave for ten days."

"That reminds me, said Blaine, fishing in his own pockets. "Here are some photos, maps and so on that I got from those two dead Germans, Bauer and his pilot. They may be of service up at headquarters."

And he handed them over, Buck supplementing them with a few he too had taken on his various ventures within the last day or two.

CHAPTER 19

Conclusion

Two days later a couple of rather spruce looking young men alighted from an eastern train in Paris and, strolling forth in the crowd of passengers, looked about them rather curiously.

Both had passed through the French capital before, but more as strangers and foreigners than as ally Americans, visiting a city famed as the centre of all that is best in French history and tradition.

"Looks much like little old New York," remarked Buck, "only I don't see so many skyscrapers."

"I like that!" said Blaine. "I never did fall in love with fifty-story shacks that seem to resent the sunlight down here below. I wish Stan could be with us, don't you?"

"Yep! But I bet he's satisfied with the nursing he's getting off that pretty Chicago girl we left him with. What we better do? Wait for something to happen?"

"'Looks that way. Our wire said for us to wait at the depot." And Blaine, looking curiously around, happened to be turned the wrong way when a uniformed porter came up to Bangs, touched his cap and said:

"Pardon, messieurs, but will you come with me?" And be presented a card upon which was engraved the name of Senator Walsen. Under this was hastily pencilled in a feminine hand: "We are waiting. Please follow the porter." That was all.

Buck, slightly confused, tugged at Blaine's sleeve, saying:

"Come on! They're waiting for us—somewhere."

With a start of surprise Blaine obeyed, and each bearing his hand-bag, they set out dumbly after the station official who had already picked up a couple of suit-cases.

For a minute or more they threaded the mixed throngs of civilians, officials, soldiers of all grades and many nationalities, together with trainmen, guards, gendarmes and what not, to a line of waiting cabs, taxies, motor-cars just beyond a series of high iron gates. At one of these a sentry, together with a railway official, examined their tickets, and more important still their passes or permits. After this, both sentry and guard, respectfully saluting, stood aside and the porter took them to a big grey limousine drawn up near by. A uniformed driver sat in front, while the porter placed the luggage in a rear rack and climbed up behind himself.

All this was comparatively unnoticed, for the door opened and two lovely faces peered out as the young men came up.

Just then Blaine felt unduly conscious of one or more court-plastered places upon his cranial anatomy, while Buck felt that a wound or two on arm and neck somehow detracted from his natural freedom of movement. And yet neither had given the matter a thought before. These were the chances of war. Chances with ladies, however, were just then much more important.

But the two young women, charmingly dressed, were all smiles and cordiality.

"You will excuse father, won't you?" lisped Andra, while both made way inside the *tonneau* for the two to enter. There they were eagerly greeted by no less a personage than Orris Erwin, also on leave, who shook bands heartily.

In the *tonneau* were two seats, each roomy enough for three. As the car started on, all chatting eagerly, Avella supplemented Andra's remark with:

"Papa had to attend some kind of a war meeting at Versailles. He deputized us to welcome you., Mr. Erwin insisted oncoming, too."

"Why, this is great, great!" enthused Blaine, his awkwardness all gone under the cordiality of this greeting. "I always wanted to get leave, you know. So did Buck. Orry seems to have got in ahead on the leave business."

He grinned at Erwin, but Andra put in with:

"Well, we're all on leave only, aren't we, Mr. Erwin?"

"You gir—you ladies, too?" essayed Bangs, while Erwin nodded.

"Why, yes. We're enlisted in the Red Cross, you know, and they're so strict about letting us off. But we, too, got our ten days. It will give us time to show you boys about the city a bit. And we're so glad you got back safe and are in time. Besides, tonight is going to be the big time for you boys."

"You are right, Vella." Andra smiled roguishly. "Mr. Erwin has been so curious. He's always wanting to know."

Clearly something was up, but recognizing that good manners were now a point to be duly considered, the young men managed to conquer their curiosity and confine their attention to other not less agreeable things.

They motored out to the Walsen residence, near the American Embassy, and were ensconced with Erwin in a suite of apartments much superior to what they had been used to of late.

The day passed. Senator Walsen returned. With him was the American Ambassador and a stout, elderly, yet martial looking man, already one of the most famous of the high Marshals of France, and now well known in the United States.

There was a dinner of state that evening, to which not only these three aviators were invited, but also various other French and Americans who had more or less distinguished themselves.

At the hour appointed no less a personage than the President of the French Republic, with several of his leading supporters also came. Altogether some twenty or more were assembled in the Walsen drawing-room just before the dinner hour.

Somewhat nervous, yet hopeful, our youngsters carefully prepared themselves for what Bangs confessed was "a blame sight more trying than any of the Boche scrimmages we have tackled of late."

"You are making mountains out of mole-bills; you know you are." Andra and Avella were smiling now, both doubly charming in their new Red Cross gowns.

As a matter of fact all three lads in their clean, trim aviation uniforms presented both a manly, martial and genteel appearance. At the last moment in came Captain Byers just in from the front; and with him was Stanley, pale and rather thin, yet surprisingly strong, considering his severe experiences. Miss Daskam was not there, but if one had looked closely at Stanley's pockets, the edge of a small photo of that young lady might have peeped out. Most likely this would have aroused Erwin's jealousy. Who knows?

When all were assembled and the usual round of introductions had been gone through with, Senator Walsen rose, introducing the Marshal, and concluding as follows:

"We not only love our French brothers-in-arms, but we know they love us. Our distinguished leader here," indicating the Marshal, "'wishes now to substantially prove this.'" And he gave way to the great Frenchman, who motioned to our lads to stand up, and then proceeded to pin on each young breast a cross of honour, bestowed for gallantry on the west front.

Directly Captain Byers also came forward and read an order from our War Department authorizing the General commanding our forces in France to declare the following promotions:

Lafayette Blaine to be First Lieutenant in the new American Aviation corps, Buck Bangs to be Second Lieutenant in same; and Orris Erwin and George Stanley to be First Sergeants. Effect to be immediate. Also furloughs granted to each for ten days at full pay.

Then the Marshal, whose command of English was limited, briefly yet succinctly complimented them all, especially Captain Byers, who had just come back from the line pressing the retiring enemy.

After that, of course, there was nothing to do but announce the dinner.

"How do you feel after all this?" curiously asked Andra Walsen of Blaine while waiting for a succeeding course in the rather stately march of the repast. "Do you feel good?"

"I always feel best when you are with me," he simply replied.

"Oh!" she replied, and there was unwonted colour in her face as she looked down at a rose he had given her, now pinned right over her heart.

Both Buck and Avella looked quite as if they had been discussing the fact that, after all, were they not natural neighbours? Was not she from Idaho—he from Montana? What more would anybody have?

And so let us leave them. The war still goes on, grows in bitterness, fierceness, cruelty, all or mostly inaugurated by Fritz the Hun.

How neat, how appropriate the name!

Let us, good reader, hope that if these young folks do survive the war and return to their homes alive, that some of their dawning dreams may come true, despite the Hun and all his works.